The Abiding Questions

of

Free Congregations

The Abiding Questions

of

Free Congregations

The Meadville Lombard Reader

Volume II

Sermons and essays from the
Meadville Lombard Theological School
community during 2006

Edited by Susann Pangerl, PhD

Meadville Lombard Press
Chicago, Illinois

The Abiding Questions of Free Congregations: The Meadville Lombard Reader Volume II
Edited by Rev. Susann Pangerl Ph.D.
Copyright ©2007 by Meadville Lombard Theological School

First Edition 2007

Meadville Lombard Press
5701 S. Woodlawn Avenue
Chicago, IL 60637

Cover design and cover art by Marian Stewart

ISBN: 0-9795589-1-3
ISBN: 978-0-9795589-1-7

Library of Congress Number: 2007941102

Printed in the United States of America

ABIDING QUESTIONS OF FREE CONGREGATIONS:

An Introduction

Unitarian Universalism is a questioning faith. Hence it is appropriate that the title of this second Meadville Lombard Reader is, *The Abiding Questions of a Free Church*, taken from Alice Blair Wesley's essay contribution of the same title. This attitude of a questioning faith captures well the tenor of the essays and sermons chosen for inclusion in this volume. The essays and sermons that follow were selected from a wealth of submissions from the Meadville Lombard community. The selections reflect the generational reach and locations of our ministries. The authors include Meadville Lombard faculty, recent graduates, those seasoned in ministry and those in various stages of ministerial preparation, and Canadians as well as Americans. The occasions for the writing of these pieces varied. Some were written for conference presentations. Others were written as class assignments. Still others reflect the voices of our clergy on Sunday mornings.

To paraphrase, H. Richard Niebuhr, a noted 20th century theologian, good theology addresses the questions of its time. The authors in this volume struggle to identify the critical ethical and religious questions which inform our religious living as Unitarian Universalists in these times. This endeavor is a deeply personal, often soul-wrenching process. It requires courage: Courage to wrestle with unsettling realities. Courage to risk seeing oneself and our faith communities realistically.

Courage to dare to ask the question "what if" with a discerning eye and open heart to the possibilities for the kinds of justice-seeking, compassionate communities we could become.

This volume is divided into two parts. Part One contains four essays. My esteemed colleague, David Bumbaugh's essay takes the long view. His essay explores the historical tensions within the United States of how the aspirations of the founders toward the creation of the United States as a virtuous republic found expression. In question is the role and function of religious communities, as semi-public institutions, as vital in the continuous task of prophetic witness and in the formation of morally responsive citizens. Alice Blair Wesley's essay raises the question of "what have we promised to do together religiously?" She searches to identify for us "the ways of the holy" within the patterns and practices of free church life. She challenges us to analyze the "patterns of face-to-face interaction with one another" in which we discover where and how the holy appears.

David Pyle's essay raises the question of how Unitarian Universalism makes active its principles in the daily lives of its individual members. He turns to the Buddhist precepts as his vehicle of exploration. The final essay by Tracy Springberry offers a personal essay on her personal search for a theological grounding able to sustain her deeply humanist sensibilities and reliance in human reason and experience. She finds in the works of Henry Nelson Wieman the beginnings of this theological understanding.

The essays in part one raise critical questions for our consideration. How do we form moral citizens within the space of our religious communities? How do we nurture the holy in the face-to-face interactions? What is civic virtue? What is the reach of our collective moral vision for our society and its policies? Part two contains eight sermons. These sermons offer, by example, particular answers to these questions. The first five sermons illustrate their theological wrestling with provocative images of walls, roads, hiding, belonging, sunflowers and ooze. These images are the stuff of practical theology being written in new voices. The final three sermons return us to dangerous moral challenges facing us in these days. The manner in which we respond will be the measure of our contributions to this nation as a virtuous republic.

Rev. Susi Pangerl Ph.D.

November, 2007

CONTENTS

Part One:
The Essays

Religion and the Virtuous Republic

David E. Bumbaugh, BD '64
Professor of Ministry

Chautauqua Institution

July 12, 2006

In 1787, as the Constitutional Convention was finishing its epic work, Benjamin Franklin was confronted by a woman who wanted to know, "Well, Doctor, what kind of government have we got, a monarchy or a republic?" Franklin paused a moment and then responded, "A republic, if you can keep it."

Franklin's response reflected a deeply shared skepticism both within the Convention and outside it about the ability of the new nation to function for long as a republic. While there was much agreement about the advantages of the republican system, there was equal concern about the ability of a republican form of government to survive over time and about whether it was sustainable in a nation that was geographically extensive and intentionally expansive.

The history of republican government suggested that it was most successful in small, monocultural, geographically contained city-states. There was little experience with the republican model in states extending over vast geographical distances and incorporating a citizenry drawn from a variety of diverse cultures. More than this, the history of republics, even in city states, suggested that they were highly vulnerable to tyrannies, oligarchies and despotism, particularly in times of tension and crisis. So, on that day in 1787, good Doctor Franklin was not just coining another aphorism for Bartlett's Book of Famous Quotations; he was voicing a deep and lasting concern.

In framing the Constitution, the founders had worked mightily to guard the new government against the foreseeable weaknesses inherent in the republican system. They had established three separate and competing branches of government, on the theory that each would serve as a check on the others' inevitable efforts to arrogate too much power to themselves. They had divided the legislative branch into two houses, each with strong incentives to protect its special prerogatives against the ambitions of the other. They had provided for direct election of one house and for indirect election of the other house and of the president, intending to give the people some voice while protecting the government from transient fanaticism moving across the body politic, or, as they sometimes named it, "the mob." They had reserved important powers to the constituent states. But even this, they feared, would not be enough to guarantee that the people could keep the republic they had crafted out of a welter of argument and debate, necessity and compromise.

Behind the misgivings hidden in Franklin's comment was a deep conviction that the ultimate success of the republic would depend upon an element that could not be written into any document or hedged about by any restrictions or limitations—an element so difficult to describe that they could only point to it with a vague, metaphorical language. Coming out of the constitutional convention, the framers were possessed of a conviction that the success or failure of their work would depend upon the nation's ability to create and sustain virtuous citizens, and the literature of the time reflects this ongoing concern for how to create and sustain a virtuous citizenry.

It should be pointed out that the concept of the virtuous citizen was deeper and more profound than the simple vision of a citizen who obeyed the law, who was trustworthy in his or her dealings, who would meet obligations and responsibilities with personal integrity. All of this was important, but the concept of virtuous citizenship pointed beyond this kind of basic personal morality. Virtuous citizenship was rooted in a vision that was not limited to personal ethics but embraced an ethic of public and civic virtue—a deep and abiding concern for the commonweal, an unshakable commitment to the greater good, a concern for more than the immediate moment, a willingness to act beyond personal or partisan advantage, an embrace of the obligations that emerge from a sense of living responsibly in relation to that which is larger and more important and more lasting than the struggles for immediate gain and transient advantage. The founding generation was convinced that this kind of citizenship was essential if the republic that had been created was to be kept. It was this kind of citizenship that Washington and others appealed to in their frequent admonitions to avoid political parties and divisive partisanship.

The new republic was not very old before it became clear that even the best of men would be tempted to slide into the abyss of faction and enlist in partisan struggles. It was soon clear the new republic could not avoid partisanship and therefore, it could not, in the midst of day to day struggles for advantage, function as the nursery from which virtuous citizens might arise. If the republic was going to produce the virtuous citizens upon which its survival depended, it would have to find some way to nurture and shape the young apart from the seductive and corrupting quotidian struggles of the world of politics and commerce. That task would be centered within the home. In the home, kept clear of the rough and tumble of the outside world, children would learn the abiding virtues upon which the republic rested. The primary teachers of these virtues of republican citizenship would be, of course, the mothers of the nation. And thus was born the concept that Linda Kerber calls the cult of Republican Motherhood.

As early as 1776, Abigail Adams, in a letter to her husband, John, had admonished him to "remember the ladies" as he set out on his treasonous course of nation-building, warning her absent husband that women would not willingly assent to a new government in which they were subjected to patriarchal despotism. Despite the prodding of a handful who dared to dream that the revolution would mean greater scope for the talents of women, the document that emerged from the Constitutional Convention did not "remember the ladies." However, the need to produce and nurture virtuous citizens conferred upon women a very important, indeed, a central, if unofficial, role in the destiny of the new nation, and many women embraced that responsibility without reservation. They saw their exclusion from the political and economic life of the nation not as a burden but as a necessary condition if they were to fulfill their special duty to the republic.

This may help explain a often forgotten event in the early history of the nation. In 1776, New Jersey adopted a new constitution that granted suffrage to all citizens of the state who were of age and who possessed an estate worth 50 pounds. This was not universal suffrage, the truly poor, indentured servants, slaves and others could not vote, but under this constitution, persons of property, white and black, men and women were permitted to vote and many availed themselves of that right until 1807. In that year, responding to charges of voting irregularities in an election to decide the location of the Essex County courthouse, the state revised its voting laws, restricting the franchise to white males. The curious thing is that though women had been voting for three decades, there was little or no public reaction on the part of women to this abrupt change in their status. I would suggest that many women had fully embraced the cult of Republican Motherhood, and the conviction that engagement in the political process, in fact, threatened their ability to maintain a household that was free from the corrosive effects of entanglement with the outside world. The surrender of the right to cast a ballot every few years was a price they were prepared to pay for the ability to fulfill their larger political responsibility to the republic.

This notion that virtue could be nurtured best in institutions and settings free from involvement in the rough and tumble of political and economic activity may help explain the concern for separation of church and state in the early republic. It is often argued that underlying the drive for separation of church and state was a fear of religious conflict and a concern that the state might be corrupted by the temptation of ecclesiastical authorities to use the power of the state to coerce belief. While those concerns were frequently expressed, the fact remains that various states had long had established churches and, indeed, disestablishment would not be completed until Massachusetts ended its entanglement with religion in 1833. It was also clear that even in those states with an established church, dissenting groups early gained a foothold and soon were much too strong to be dislodged. While there often had been significant religious debate and disagreement, there had been little serious threat of state involvement in religious conflict. For these reasons, I am inclined to attach more importance to the notion, expressed from time to time by advocates of separation, that separation of church and state was necessary in order to protect the church from corruption by the state and the political process.

If the home, insulated from the rough and tumble of the political and economic struggles of the day, was to be the nursery in which virtuous citizens would be reared, the church, freed from entanglement with the politics of the state, would be that institution which would continue to call its adherents to virtuous behavior as citizens. Not expecting to curry political favor, religion would function to remind citizens of imperatives beyond the ethics of the main chance, beyond the struggle for immediate advantage.

It is clear from reading various of the early founders that they had little corporate commitment to specific religious dogma or doctrine. They referred to "nature and nature's God" rather than to the God of the scriptures. The Constitution, itself, never references God. Washington, at one point, remarked that he attended the Protestant service in the morning and the Catholic service in the afternoon because it was good for the people to see that religion is held in high regard. (Interestingly enough, a similar sentiment was expressed by President Eisenhower, when he insisted that "our form of government is based upon a deeply felt religious faith—and I don't care what it is.") The role of generic religion was to reinforce and sustain the early training of virtuous citizens and it would do so by recalling citizens to an ethic and a morality that was rooted in larger responsibilities and prior loyalties. That emphasis on the ethical and moral role of religion was graphically demonstrated by Thomas Jefferson's Bible—an edited, scissors and paste edition of the New Testament Gospels that excised the miraculous and interventionist stories and retained the central ethical and moral teachings of Jesus. Religion's job was to function as reinforcement to virtuous citizenship reminding citizens of abiding, overriding ethical, moral, social concerns as they contended with the immediate and transient political and economic struggles of daily life. The church, like republican mothers, was to remain pure by not, itself, engaging in those struggles.

Before long, women began to sense the crucial flaw in this central vision. By segregating a concern for moral and ethical education and nurture in the home and by segregating the realm of the home from engagement in the political life of society, the public realm had been given tacit permission to engage in behavior that was at best amoral and ethically questionable. Virtue was defined as the realm of women and children and clergy who were protected from the real world—the world of tragic but unavoidable conflict and compromise by men who managed the morally questionable public realm of politics and commerce. More than this, virtue was refocused upon personal values, rather than the larger, public concerns the founders believed critical to the success of the republic. Despite their best efforts, women knew that their sons would remain virtuous citizens, even by this narrowed definition, only so long as they were sheltered in the home and that as soon as those sons became men and entered the real world, the work of the home would be undone. Increasingly, women began to search for ways to change the world their children would confront as they left the home. The work of creating virtuous citizens would be undermined unless the world into which children emerged was, itself, a world of virtue—effective virtuous citizenship required a virtuous republic. Slowly, women emerged from the cocoon of

Republican Motherhood, and began the long struggle for social change. Beginning with the temperance campaigns of the early 1800's and moving then into concerns for women's rights, abolition, public education, prison reform, mental health reform, and an end to child labor, courageous women sought to preserve the republic by amending the world, by making it a place where virtue might flourish, not as a tender house plant, but as a sturdy and hearty native species.

It took the church longer to understand the contradictions inherent in trying to promote virtue from within a ghetto sealed off from the rough and tumble of daily life. Throughout the first half of the nineteenth century, records of church conventions are replete with minutes reporting the reluctance of the church to intrude upon or even comment upon any issue that might seem to be political or economic in nature. Repeatedly, well into the 1850's, religious bodies seem to have interpreted separation of church and state as barring religion from seeking to influence legislation or public policy. Even the greatest moral issue of the century—slavery—was regarded in many instances as a political and economic conundrum, and therefore not an appropriate subject for religious groups to address.

In time even the religious establishment came to see that virtuous citizenship not only required institutions that nurtured and supported individuals, it also required a virtuous republic in which ethical and moral values would be enacted, respected and allowed to flourish. The question of slavery, of course, was the moral dilemma that forced the recognition that abstract concern for virtue is meaningless unless it engages concrete, public issues in ways that eventuate in significant social policy. Church bodies split and divided over the issue of slavery, but north and south, pro-slavery and antislavery, the conviction that religion could not and should not address public issues was laid aside as sectional conflict grew and the horrors of the Civil War burst upon the nation. Concern for the creation of a virtuous republic grew as one legacy of that terrible conflict.

One might argue that this recognition, this willingness of the home and the church to embrace a larger social vision and to engage the public realm around that vision, is one reason that Dr. Franklin's fears have not been fully realized. Despite the increasing complexity and size of the republic he and others fashioned, the structure has proved to be remarkably strong and flexible. Women, in their struggle for a more just, humane, and enlarged social order, and the church, in its willingness to bring moral judgments to bear on political, economic and social issues created a semipublic space between the public and the private realms that allowed values and ethical concerns to become part of public discourse in this republic. Women continued to be concerned to create in the home an environment in which virtuous citizens might be shaped and molded. The church continued to be concerned to support the personal integrity that would allow individuals to withstand the contravening pressures of the world. But increasingly it became clear that the space between the private world of the home and church, and the public world of politics and economics was the locus in which moral and ethical discourse must take place.

In the years after the Civil War and continuing into the middle of the twentieth century, a significant role for many religious institutions was to provide this kind of locus for addressing public issues from a moral, ethical, even theological perspective. As the nation expanded across a continent, as exploitation of natural and human resources produced wealth unimagined by the founders, as the United States emerged upon the world stage as a major power, it was frequently the church that confronted public policy with moral imperatives. Though this was scarcely the only focus of the church, throughout the era of the social gospel, religious groups often challenged government and culture on behalf of a larger loyalty and a deeper duty. While it continued to provide comfort to the distressed, healing love to those in pain and grief, while it continued to encourage individuals in the trials of life, much of the religious community was convinced that the pastoral needs of individuals inevitably betrayed a social dimension and that the duty of religion was to confront the powers and principalities, to challenge the social structures that generated so much needless pain and grief and despair. Issues like child labor, poverty, worker justice, racial prejudice, prisoner's rights, the death penalty, issues of peace and war, economic exploitation all provided opportunities for religious leaders to confront conventional practices and behaviors and values in behalf of a larger social vision and to call the republic to virtue.

In the middle of the twentieth century, as the United States emerged from the Second World War and entered upon the shadowy struggle known as the Cold War, events conspired to refocus and re-structure the religious vision. The World War had been seen as a moral contest between good and evil, in which there was little room for con-structive criticism of those engaged in a desperate struggle for the future of the human soul. As that war was transformed into a contest with "atheistic communism," the vision of moral struggle was transferred to the new global engagement. The East-West confrontation became a con-tinuation of the struggle between good and evil, between the godly and the godless, and the pressure to identify the republic with good and with God became all but irresistible. It was in this context that we adopted "In God we trust" as our national motto, placed the language "under God" in the pledge to the flag and assumed that religion would function as a major support of the state and its policies.

While some voices in the religious community continued to protest this identification of the nation with God, the focus of much of religion was elsewhere. It was difficult for the religious community to challenge a society that was identified as the agent of God in a global struggle for the human soul, when the undoubted economic and military power of the United States seemed to indicate that the state functioned under a divine mandate. What is more, after years of global warfare, Americans were eager to get back to normal, to begin families, to create homes, to fill their lives with the abundance that had been denied them during the years of economic depression and warfare. Churches were eager to help the process. They reached out to new young families, built new churches, and refocused much of their energies into community building, and programs of salvation based on therapeutic models.

The role of the religious community as critic of the social order waned. To be sure, Martin Luther King, with his Letter from the Birmingham Jail reawakened some of the clergy and laity and as the war in Vietnam dragged on, some were driven to challenge prevailing political policies, but for the most part, the church was too deeply invested in its alliance with the state to offer the kind of sustained challenge that would provide the arena for a healthy and vibrant debate over public policy. Once more, voices were raised insisting that the church had no right to engage in politics and pressures upon religion to withdraw into the private realm increased.

What few people noticed in this process was a subtle but significant shift in the functioning of the state and the nature of American religion. While the state wrapped its policies and practices in the language of traditional religion, the very nature of the religious venture had shifted. In his book *American Theocracy*, Kevin Phillips describes the manner in which the church abandoned its role as critic of the political establishment. The liberal churches became mired in a kind of therapeutic theology that is reminiscent of the hope early in the history of the nation that by focusing on the needs and potential of the individual, virtuous citizens can be supported in their efforts to create and sustain a virtuous republic. The role of the church, from this perspective is to support and empower but not to embrace the kind of challenging engagement with social issues that might alienate lay people or endanger their status as tax-exempt institutions. On the other hand, conservative and evangelical churches have identified the nation as the appropriate vehicle for empowering their religious and apocalyptic vision. Phillips suggests that the Republican Party has become so identified with the evangelical vision that it is a de facto religious party. If Phillips is right, the Southern Baptist Convention may be seen as the Republican Party at prayer.

The effect of this identification of political policy and religious vision is two-fold. On the one hand, the kind of critical debate in which immediate policies are set against a vision of ultimate values, the kind of critical debate that is necessary for the existence of a virtuous republic is lost as transient policy decisions are defined as expressions of eternal verities and divine mandates. On the other hand, with the state empowered by a divine mandate, and endowed with vast military and economic resources, the temptation to function not as a republic but as an empire is all but irresistible. And so, the republic fashioned by Dr. Franklin and his colleagues heads down the path of imperial ambition that promises to destroy the very values upon which it was founded. Its foreign policy is focused upon the determination to achieve global hegemony; its economic policy is intended to transfer wealth from the periphery to the center, from the poor to the rich, from the many to the few; it sacrifices the reality of freedom and democracy for empty symbols. With God on its side, the United States has little need of allies, can project its choices as universally valid, can engage in endless warfare against terrorism, against a noun with little concern for collateral damage and all the while blindly stoke the growing rage and resentment of a world that refuses to acquiesce in the assertion that this nation functions as the chosen instrument of divine purpose.

"Dr. Franklin," asked a woman, "what kind of government do we have, a monarchy or a republic?"

"A Republic," replied Franklin, "if you can keep it."

The warning contained in that response has echoed down the corridors of our national history and it sounds with special meaning in our time. As we find ourselves tempted by imperial hubris, the time to act—if we are to keep the republic our forebears struggled to create—grows short. I would submit that part of what is needed is to recover a vision of the role religion can and should play in creating a virtuous republic. Religion cannot meet its responsibilities by seeking to absent itself from engagement with issues of public and social policy. Neither can it behave responsibly by identifying with the transient policies of the moment. The role of religion in creating and sustaining a virtuous republic is to constantly confront the immediate with the eternal, the transient with the abiding, the conservative with the transformative. It is not the job of religion to support any administration or its policies. It is not the job of religion to advance national interests. It is the job of religion to stand in critical judgment on administrations, on policies, on the nation itself; to cast an alternative light on the events of the moment and the policies of the day and expose the inner reality behind the public face.

There are models of this kind of religious function embedded in the western religious tradition. In the Hebrew texts the story is told of the prophet Nathan, who stood before King David and described the conduct of a rich and powerful man who coveted that which belonged to his poor neighbor. Deviously, the rich man plotted the death of that neighbor, so that he might remove the final obstacle to the fulfillment of his ambitions. King David, indignantly demanded to know who was this wicked man who so abused his power and his wealth to despoil his neighbor. Standing before the entire court, the prophet pointed his finger at the mighty king and declared for all to hear, "Thou art the man," calling the powerful monarch himself to account for his lustful abuse of power and position and privilege.

In the Hebrew texts, the story is told of Amos, a herdsman, a dresser of sycamores, who travels to the seat of government in the Kingdom of Israel. There, in a public place, he dares to call the entire nation to account for its gross misdeeds, its rapacious policies, its failed vision of the right. He declares that the God they embrace so loudly and so publically hates their feasts and their sacrifices. He declares that the nation has betrayed its duty to others, having sold the poor for silver and the needy for a pair of shoes. He calls down judgment upon a people who have allowed greed and expedience and love of power to replace the vision of righteousness and virtue that should have been enshrined at the center of their national existence.

In both of these instances, and in others, the religious vision, the ethical vision, the moral vision has confronted the politics of expediency and of power and of aggrandizement and insisted that there is a higher duty than to immediate policy and short term advantage and the ethics of the main chance. In both of these instances, there is a vision of a virtuous society—one defined by a deep and abiding concern for the commonweal, an unshakable commitment to the greater good, a concern for more than the immediate moment, a willingness to act beyond personal or partisan advantage, an embrace of the obligations that emerge from a sense of living responsibly in relation to that which is larger and more important and more lasting than struggles for immediate gain and transient advantage. It is this vision that religion is called to serve; it is in light of this vision that religion is required to call powers and principalities to account; it is in behalf of this vision that religion is charged to engage the political realm in service to the dream of a virtuous republic.

In this age of fundamentalist fanaticism, however, religion has another critical role to play, one that sometimes seems contradictory—the role of reminding human beings of the inevitable limitations of any vision or understanding we find compelling. In the book of Isaiah and scattered throughout the religious texts of our culture, we are cautioned, over and over again, to embrace our finitude, to understand that God's ways are not our ways, nor are our thoughts God's thoughts. In a recent essay, a contemporary prophet, Wendell Berry, makes a compelling plea for what he calls the "way of ignorance." Berry reminds us that all our knowing, all our wisdom, all our convictions float in a vast sea of ignorance and misconception; that what we don't know, what we don't understand, what we cannot envision may be more important than all of our highly attested competencies and brightly burnished truths. Berry reminds us that behind all our brave assertions about the world, about truth, and about justice lie profound unasked, indeed, often half-formed questions. In light of that reality, he suggests, we are driven to embrace humility and mercy as the cardinal human virtues. He does not ask us to abandon our search for truth nor does he challenge the importance of facts, but he does ask us to embrace our finitude, to understand the limitations that are built into every fact and every truth we find, and every vision we embrace, and to make our necessary judgments with a consistent spirit of humility.

The duty of religion in an age of fundamentalist certainty is to call the republic to humility, while demanding attention to underlying values and deeper loyalties than party or nation, to do so with a sense of proportion reminding the body politic that it is not God's agent on earth, that it is not the embodiment of eternal and unvarying and indisputable truth.

This is, perhaps, the most critical role religion can play in our contemporary efforts to keep the republic we have inherited—to resist the temptation to engage the power of the state in behalf of compelling, but inevitably limited and flawed religious visions. A virtuous republic cannot survive in a climate in which religion becomes an instrument of the state or the state functions as an instrument of religion. The role of religion is to maintain its independence, to create a separate, semipublic space in which policies may be judged, may be debated, not in terms of their pragmatic consequences, but in terms of their ethical, moral consequences; a semipublic space in which the imperatives of the moment may be confronted by long-term implications; a semipublic space in which humility functions to call us back from attempts to preempt the future, in which concern for a common humanity confronts expediency with the human face of collateral damage.

"A republic, if you can keep it," said Benjamin Franklin. Whether we can keep it is a question that confronts every generation. Can we structure a republic in which virtue is honored and rewarded, in which virtue is a public as well as a private matter, in which virtuous citizens embrace an ethic of public and civic virtue—a deep and abiding concern for the commonweal, an unshakable commitment to the greater good, a concern for more than the immediate moment, a willingness to act beyond personal or partisan advantage, an embrace of the obligations that emerge from a sense of living responsibly in relation to that which is larger and more important and more lasting than the struggles for immediate gain and transient advantage?

The founders were right. The republic cannot survive without virtuous citizens. Over time we have learned that personal virtue cannot be effective and consequential outside the context of a virtuous republic.

Calling the republic to virtue is the ethical, moral, theological responsibility of religion, of all those who are concerned for the future of the republic, of all those who take religion seriously.

The Abiding Questions of Free Congregations

Alice Blair Wesley, ISP '77

Delivered, by invitation, to the UUA Board of Trustees

October 20, 2006

Most of us have known moments of overflowing love, "when a new light has seemed to dawn, a new life to stir within us." That we have such moments is part of what it means to be human. Moreover, as Wm. Ellery Channing said, "It is on this part of our nature that religion is founded. (Discourse at the Dedication of Divinity Hall, Cambridge, 1826)

Yet scattered individual moments don't yield the hope of authentic religion, either for us or for the world. Authentic religion grows out of, evolves from, many deeply personal moments of overflowing love. These moments happen often when we gather often, every Sabbath, on purpose to heed and "think on whatsoever things are true, honorable, just, lovely and of good report." (Phil. 4) When we heed these things often, with a faithful body of others, we drink as from a fountain of living water that renews and strengthens and sustains authentic religious love.

We don't "do church" to bypass or repress or fix less desirable or defective parts of human nature. We do church to see to the most vital part, our thirst to admire and love all that is worthy of dedicated living, to keep first things first, in our hearts and minds and lives. The issue is not: Is human nature good or bad? The issue is: What is human nature's most vital part, and in what social patterns can we keep this part at the center of our lives, where it belongs?

The whole purpose of a rightly covenanted free church is to lift up worthy realities so that—hearing of them in story and song, "seeing" them, pondering them, reflecting on them together—we respond with the grace of love. The good news is any group of people who regularly lift up worthy realities and reason together concerning the ways of love and try to live in these ways, will thrive and draw new members into the covenant with them. Thriving free churches are the best hope of the world. For any one of them may become like a raised candlestick that gives light to the whole house, like a city set on a hill that cannot be hid, like a beacon showing many the way away from death and destruction unto life and life abundant. That you and I derive from people whose doctrine of the church this was nearly four centuries ago, is the reason we are gathered here now on Beacon Hill.

Free church hope does not lie in "the inherent worth and dignity of every person." It lies in the ongoing dynamic of events in the life of any ongoing, faithfully covenanted group. Individuality flourishes in such a group, for sure. More important historically is that many abroad will benefit from what goes on there, when members keep first things first. In our tradition we call these groups free churches. Certainly, there have been and are similar groups in all traditions, whatever they are called. All are part of "the church universal."

I cite the first and last line of perhaps the most often recited version, among us, of the free church covenant.

> *Love is the doctrine of this church. . .*
> *Thus do we covenant with one another and with God.*
> *(L. Griswold Williams, Singing the Living Tradition,*
> *#471)*

Covenanted, we have entered a glad, oft renewed promise with others to live freely together, insofar as we are able, in accordance with dynamic laws of reality that make our freedom possible. A covenant is based in a shared understanding of human nature and features of the interdependent web of existence of which we are a part, or, that reality greater than all yet present in each. "God" is a shorter name for "the One" who makes the interdependent web what it is and human nature what it is within the web. For reasons long to explain, some of us can't use that shorter name, which is all right with those of us who do.

We need often to ask each other in our congregations: What have our members promised—implicitly or explicitly—to do together religiously? In what patterned practices, or programs, do we go about doing these things? And who decides what we shall do together and how?

These are our questions of "faith and order." Our tradition prescribes, not answers but, core questions—abiding questions. We are united in authentic religion when we answer them together, try living out our answers, and ask them again, over and again. Thus does every generation earn our heritage and sing our Living Tradition, with the ages.

Some say our questions have no right or wrong answers. That is not true. Answers that bind us are flexible, like a strong rubber band. Limp, a rubber band holds nothing within its flabby boundary. It holds things together when it is stretched, in tension. Stretched more, it holds more. Stretched too far, it breaks and holds nothing. Our answers do—and must—fall within a flexible but real boundary.

Other abiding questions of local congregations:

> *How shall we worship?*
>
> *What shall we teach, especially our children and new members?*
>
> *How shall we train and support our lay and ordained leaders?*
>
> *How shall we do justice and mercy?*

How could we help a new congregation get started well?

And how shall we give and take counsel, on all these matters, with other UU congregations, especially those near us?

Two misconceptions, it seems to me, contribute to our present awful weakness. One is a too narrow notion of the meaning of congregational polity, which omits a crucial sense of obligation to give and take counsel with neighboring congregations. The other is the absurd notion that free congregations could ever be much helped by a UUA which is at once casual about the meaning of member congregations' participation and hierarchical in its governance structure.

Here I'll tell a story. It's not true. I made it up.

There was a little UU congregation of almost 70 members with a church school of 15 or 20 children. With a new minister, they began to grow. Within two years they had about 100 members and, routinely, more than 70 kids in church school. Their building lot was tiny. Leading members saw they were just going to have to raise the money, buy new land and erect a new building. A UU church not too far away had completed a new sanctuary only a year or two ago. So the board chair of the little church picked up the phone and called this other board chair.

He said, "Say! You raised a lot of money to put up your new place. Would 3 or 4 of your capital campaign folks come up and tell us how you did it? We've got to learn how."

She said, "Sure. When do you want us to come?" This other board chair and the whole capital campaign committee came to meet with the small church board. After the pleasantries, she said, "What are you people doing up here to draw so many kids? We have 270 members, but we don't get 70 children."

He said, "Well, tell you what. You teach us to raise money; we'll show you how we've learned to do RE."

She said, "Deal! We were wondering if your RE committee would come down and meet with our board and RE committee. How soon could you come?"

And the RE committee did go down and meet with the others three times, while folks at home were learning to raise money. You could call that a "he said/she said/they all did" story.

Why do you think such a story hardly ever—if ever—happens among our congregations? Why can't you hyper-active UUs, who know what goes on in churches all over the country, each tell ten true stories like unto it? Why, when it was such a struggle for me to work with a deeply troubled church, did I never think of asking three neighboring boards to meet with our board for half a day three times a year, until we got on firmer ground? Hearing wise advice on numerous matters from a phalanx of neighboring church leaders would have helped immensely! Why, as I have heard, did neighboring churches raise a lot of money for the new church in Dallas/Ft. Worth, and then leave its young officers to sink or swim without their continuing counsel? Why didn't three boards covenant to meet with them four times a year for three years, always gently to ask how things were going and to teach good patterns they themselves had used?

My short answer: many patterns of our UU Association are lousy. They may well be the biggest reason we have so many weak and small churches. Teaching by example and counsel does not much circulate among our churches, in and through our local lay and ordained leadership teams. Our leaders in the same area don't get together readily, as needed. In fact, neighboring lay leaders will most likely never even know one another's names. Some, in some years, go somewhere far off to a District Annual Meeting or General Assembly, and even attend the same "workshops." Still, their paths will never personally merge. So, how did we ever get such lousy patterns of association? That is a long, but true story. I'll give a thumbnail account of it, following this introduction.

The theological question for our kind of churches is not creedal, not, "What do we believe?" And it's not either, "What principles do we affirm?" The really big theological question of a free church is: What are the ways of love for surpassingly worthy realities in the many varying circumstances of our lives? Call the finding of these ways "the holy" of free church life. So, a central issue in the free church tradition is: In what patterns of face-to-face interaction with one another can we hope to find the ways of love—figure them out, test them in our own experience and, when we forget, remember again the ways of love? Or put the question this way: Where and how does the holy happen in the patterns of a social organization, a congregation?

If I am finding the right words, you see why in our tradition we can never properly separate the kind of freely covenanted churches ours are supposed to be from how, in what patterns, we organize. The basic agreement of a free congregation is a covenant. A covenant begins, "We covenant—or we promise—or we pledge ___." The next word is an infinitive verb form, because joining a free church is promising faithfully to do—not believe—do certain really important things with others. A social group cannot do anything, except in commonly understood and accepted patterns. The same is true when we move from talking about a congregation (singular) to an Association of Congregations (plural). A central issue is: In all the varying circumstances of congregations' lives, where and how does the holy happen as our congregations interact? Or, where and how does the holy happen in the commonly understood and accepted patterns of our Association?

Whether we use more verbs or more nouns when we talk about our patterns is very important. E.g., check out these two sentences:

#1 "We need a more effective Association."

#2 "We need to associate more effectively."

Hear #1, and what do you imagine happening? I imagine an executive boss, a CEO adding new staff or shuffling job descriptions on an organization chart. Hear #2, and what do you imagine? I imagine UUA board members calling on all our congregational board members to meet and focus together on an important specific subject, and then talk about this with still other church members—because we need to decide soon what we will do in this area. Which scenario is more typical in our Association, #1 or #2?

Frankly, we religious liberals have never had a widely shared agreement—a covenant—concerning effective and workable patterns of interaction and cooperation among our churches. If we did, our covenant might go like this:

We, members of our member congregations, covenant faithfully to send annually, for two or three days, our elected lay and ordained officers to give and take counsel concerning the state of our congregations, that assembled, our officers might together adopt, as wisely as they can, specific programs for strengthening and growing our congregations. We pledge further our financial support for programs of our Association, to the extent required by vote of our Congregational Officers in Assembly.

Churches entered into such a covenant as that would almost surely be strengthened and grow. But there's no such thing in our Unitarian or Universalist or Unitarian Universalist history. Reading only our institutional history, one would think we must be among not the brightest but the dumbest of people, who couldn't organize their way out of a paper bag. Why? It makes sense to me to understand our institutional story like this.

When our Puritan founders arrived here in New England, they had had it up to here with the hierarchical governance structures of the Church of England. All they had wanted there, really, was freedom to have informal conferences, in which groups of clergy and laity from different parishes could freely gather sometimes, hear some good preaching, pray, study and talk. But hierarchical royal rulers and bishops would have none of that. Ministerial conferees were re-assigned, demoted and silenced, or prosecuted, maybe exiled; lay conferees ordered to stay home; and a very creative variety of conferences shut down—for decades. Hierarchical control varied in amount; it never ceased. At times it was very harsh.

So, by the time 20,000 Puritans got here, in the 1630s, they were radical Congregationalists all, because by that time, they had all, clergy and lay, thought a lot about institutional structures. They needed no

"Commission on Governance" report. The Cambridge Platform of 1648 was a written summary of very wide, years-long discussion, later adopted by formal vote of every single, or distinct, congregation, unanimously.

We use the terms, Conference and Business Meeting. Our Puritan founders did not use these terms. I will use them to try to make clear what they learned, from hard experience and much study and discussion, to see as the proper distinction in patterns of association that will—over the long haul—greatly strengthen free churches. Conferences are for the giving and taking of counsel; anyone can confer. Business Meetings are for the making of group decisions; groups need by common consent to agree on who has authority to make which decisions. Conferences do not govern. Business Meetings govern.

Members of our earliest churches elected, voted, in a Business Meeting to delegate their pulpit to one or two ministers and charged each to speak truth in love from it, as he could not but see it, not as all in attendance must believe. So, in a free church with a free pulpit and free pews, even a worship service was a formally gathered Conference for the giving and taking of counsel concerning the ways of love. So as well, were all other formal and informal patterns of interaction in the church, except when a Business Meeting of covenanted members was in session. Most of the time, the congregational life of members, children, youth and non-members was, then, a special kind of self-contained and ongoing Conference. A Business Meeting was called when members of one distinct congregation needed officially to decide what they would do together. The genius of their covenantal polity was a total ban on any other governing Business Meetings whatsoever among any but covenanted members of a local church. This meant, effectively, no ecclesiastic hierarchy anywhere. None ruling a congregation (singular); none ruling over congregations (plural).

But hear this! Our founders never supposed local congregations could thrive as isolated enclaves. How could they? They never would have recovered this biblical polity and worked it out for themselves, had they not gathered in England, despite the bishops' ceaseless efforts to thwart them, in hundreds and hundreds of Conferences—now small, now larger, now here, now there, sometimes public, sometimes illegal-and-secret Conferences among ordained and lay members of many different parishes, and many professors and graduates of Puritan-dominated Cambridge University.

The Cambridge Platform of 1648 describes the many ways in which free congregations here in New England—who, of course, cared about one another's welfare—would give and take counsel, usually in informally arranged Conferences among people of various churches. They helped one another tangibly, too, as when, e.g., a church lent its Officers to a new church for as long as year.

They did have two types of formally arranged, decision-making Conferences, called Councils and Synods, each comprised of elected lay and ordained congregational Officers. A troubled, conflicted church could call for a Council meeting of Officers from several neighboring churches. A Council of officers met, listened to local members tell of their trouble, then met separately by themselves to decide what jointly to recommend the troubled church do. The Council went home. Then church members met in their own Business Meeting to decide whether or not to adopt the Council's recommendations.

Very occasionally, the congregations (plural) determined that they needed wise advice on matters affecting all of them. A Synod was called. Elected Officers attended. A Synod met, and Officers jointly decided what actions to recommend to all the churches. The Synod went home. Then members of each church met, in its own Business Meeting, officially to decide whether or not to adopt the Synod's recommendations.

So, New England free churches had lots and lots of very helpful formal and informal Conferences among congregations by which they helped one another a lot—with no hierarchy. Those were excellent patterns. Nearly all the churches using them grew large and strong, including those from whom some would eventually leave to found Universalist churches, and those that would eventually become Unitarian churches. But 170 years is a long time. By 1800 or so, religious liberals had forgotten the theological importance of widely and carefully agreed upon patterns of interaction.

From their beginnings, Universalists fussed and argued interminably over who had what authority in a tangle of variously overlapping "jurisdictions" of Business Meetings. Universalists also had humongous Conferences, all informally structured, meaning anybody and everybody could participate. Over time, those attending large Conferences adopted in Business Meeting portions of these same informally gathered Conferences ever longer and more ambitious lists of things Universalists were supposed to do out in the world, as their congregations declined ever more steeply. At last the Superintendent of the UCA was a "general with very few troops."

On the other side of our story, Unitarian churches were by the early 1800s so well established, large and strong in their small, easily traversed geographical area, that Channing, for example, said churches were just natural institutions, meaning they do not require any humanly-created patterns of interaction: churches just are. He and most Unitarians feared ecclesiastical hierarchy as much as ever, but they no longer had a theology of church organization. Unitarians had occasional Conferences, though never anything as large as the Universalists'.

The tiny AUA, organized in 1825, was all Business; its individual members just wanted to plant new churches out West. They hardly did much, because people only gave the AUA dribs and drabs of money. But a wee part-time volunteer staff kept plugging away, at least selling books and pamphlets, for 40 years. Slowly, over that 40 years, the little AUA bureaucracy accrued some informal authority, never delegated to it by the churches. It was just handy to rely on the AUA staff to do this and that. Never ever—until 1865—did Unitarians have any equivalent to a Synod, a gathering of church leaders to recommend programs which each church would vote up or down in its own Business Meeting. In 1865 the National Conference of Unitarian Churches was organized. Mostly church Officers—many more lay than ordained—attended its annual Conference-type meetings, and raised a mind-blowing amount of money for the first time. But instead of asking the churches to vote on plans to spend all that money, the N.C., at its birth, simply handed the money to the AUA board Business Meetings. In our time that would be like taking all the fair share contributions from all our churches and giving the whole kit and caboodle to one District chalice lighter committee.

The differently structured AUA and NC officially merged 1925, under the older name, AUA. All the decision-making power stayed in the Business Meetings of a tiny group of individuals. Business Meetings of a small board swallowed Conferences. As for the old pattern of Councils, decades earlier the newspapers had been full of a scandal concerning a Council, thanks to the shenanigans of John Pierpont and Theodore Parker. Unitarians were so embarrassed they abandoned without discussion that 200 year-old pattern. No Unitarian church ever called another Council.

The (new) AUA and UCA consolidated to become the UUA in 1961. Early on, UUs tried for—what many hoped would be—an appropriate separation of Conferences and Business Meetings in our annual gatherings. Even in the late '60s delegate notebooks said on the front "General Assembly and Conference." The Assembly was a Business Meeting, all other events a Conference. But we couldn't keep the distinction, and we went into decline. Since 1969, so far as most UUs are concerned, Conferences have swallowed Business Meetings. For most attendees, "GAs" are Conferences, during which, for some strange reason, some oddly keep attending those boring sessions called Business Meetings, though they're not. Nothing of significance is decided there. Of course, there are real Business Meetings somewhere. Most congregational Officers know almost nothing of what goes on in them. Nor do members of our churches vote whether or not to adopt any measures or policies coming out of them.

Recently, one of our ministers said a light bulb had gone off in his head. "GAs are our UU version of Revival Meetings!"

Do we have a modern equivalent of the old Councils? Suppose leaders in one church see conflict looming. A few members really want to get rid of the minister, though most would be happy to have her stay. So who is called in to give counsel? Lay and ordained leaders from several neighboring churches? Ah, no! Two people come, the Good Offices Person, elected by the District UUMA Chapter, and the District Executive, appointed jointly by the District board and the UUA staff. These two meet—not with all the members in an open meeting—but confidentially, with a few. Most will not even know of these meetings. The DE may advise the minister to leave "for the good of the church," lest a few stir up a damaging church fight. The GOP then will pressure the board to pay an ample severance package. Many members will never know what happened or why their minister left.

Who thinks the complicated secrecy of this pattern better than Council meetings Unitarians just dropped 150 years ago?

The old pattern was based on trust that members of neighboring churches will—certainly more often than not—elect wise Officers, and trust that members of a local church have enough collective wisdom to tell good advice from poor. Our present pattern—which, so far as I know, no Assembly ever voted to adopt—undermines trust in all directions, takes power away from elected Officers and the majority of members, and increases the power of dissidents. Mightn't we do well seriously to reflect on the patterns of our earliest churches?

For sure we can't go back to any earlier "world," and wouldn't if we could. That doesn't mean a serious look back couldn't help us choose better patterns for going forward.

My recommendations: We need to separate Conferences from Business Meetings and this time get it right. This might be an excellent time to do it, since we now have so many Conference-type "delegates" at GAs who have clearly demonstrated—they don't want to attend Business Meetings. Maybe we need "Revivals." Fine. Let's have more "Revivals." Let's have at least one major Conference in every District every summer, open to whoever has the money and interest to come, and as varied and exciting as GAs are now, only clearly called Conferences or Summer Institutes.

Our congregational Officers need to gather in less expensive, shorter, more focused and far more effective Assemblies which truly are Business Meetings, with only lay and ordained Officers of Member Congregations in attendance, there to discuss programs of our Association which they choose, and in the following years evaluate.

I read recently in a report to the UUA board on growth, "We don't need more programs. We have good programs. We need a Revival." I disagree. We need growth programs designed in broad outline by congregational Officers, not staff-designed programs which District people have then to try to "sell" or talk our churches into. For this is a kind of natural law: Free churches resist or ignore pressure coming from an ecclesiastic hierarchy. It is in our theological genes to do so. Besides, what we need is a growth program of neighborhood teams of lay and ordained leaders to give and take counsel together, learning as they go how to make a growth—or any other—program work well. We'll get such a thing only if all—and I mean all—our elected leaders talk it through and work it out together.

I believe you dear mightily working UUA board members could get leaders of our churches to associate way more effectively. I would like the board to start tomorrow to get the e-mail addresses of every elected Officer of each Member Congregation. "UUs in general" are not your proper constituency. Your proper constituents are the board members of member congregations. After each UUA board meeting, send them a brief, 2-page letter by e-mail. "Dear Congregational Officer: We will vote on the following motions at our next UUA board meeting. (List them.) To date we have considered these pro and cons of each. (List them.) We invite your board's joint comment. Please have your board Secretary send it to the UUA board Secretary. (None from individuals, please.) We certainly shall take account of your advice as we move toward a decision. Sincerely, the UUA Board of Trustees."

Please don't drown people with more information than they could possibly use. Just trying to scan all the stuff on the UUA web site, people get a bad case of attention deficit disorder.

Meanwhile, I'd like to see the UUA board make sure that on every Assembly (Business Meeting) agenda, are at least two or three items having to do with programs being planned for use in our churches—either all the churches or a special class of churches—whether they have to do with RE or growth or conflict resolution or whatever. Follow the same procedure concerning Assembly agenda items with the Officers of all our member congregations' boards. Tell them, concisely, what programs are under consideration, and about hopes for and arguments against these programs. Ask for joint board comment. Take account of what they say, and show that you do.

As for what we once called "non-business" resolutions on large social justice issues: We can have meaningful votes on these. We need to erase all those complicated rules about who can or cannot propose them. Just say they must come from at least 5 congregational boards of any one District and must—after any Assembly vote—be voted upon by member congregations in their own Business Meetings, to be considered UUA resolutions. If a "non-business" resolution receives an affirmative vote from 60% of our member Congregations, weighted by membership, it is a UUA resolution; otherwise not.

Religious love is a response to worthy realities. Religious responsibility is a response we can feel rising in us when, in good patterns, our responsibility is clearly called for. How does the holy happen in the patterns of our Association? I suggest, in patterns like these.

Living the Principles through the Precepts

Zen Buddhism: Tradition, Encounter, and Transformation

David Pyle
Student

Final Paper for Zen Buddhism: Tradition, Encounter & Transformation

When I came to Unitarian Universalism several years ago, I felt a longing for a sense of solidity. I wanted to find a guide to life and my actions within it, and, at first, I thought the seven principles might be able to provide that. Yet, before even realizing that they were meant to apply to congregations and not directly to me, I realized that they were too broad to be an effective guide to daily life.

In our efforts to ensure the freedom of our faith, we have neglected one of the primary responsibilities of human religion: to make that religion and its principles valid and active in the daily life of the adherents of the faith. Nowhere within the common conception of Unitarian Universalism are there practical guides for how to live a life that is positive, productive, and life affirming. Nowhere is there a guide for how to live a life balanced within the "web of all existence of which we are a part." We do not promote any guidelines as to how to "affirm and promote the inherent worth and dignity of every person."

My mind goes back to the young woman, a long-time Unitarian Universalist, who was helping me facilitate a UU Newcomer's group. She said to those exploring our faith, with great conviction, that in order to be a Unitarian Universalist, you have to live the seven principles in your daily life.

Before I could step in to say this was not true, one of our newcomers looked up and said, "Well how in the world do you do that? These principles are so vague I would have no idea how to live them in my daily life." That was the last time we saw him in our church.

Without some way to provide a practical guide to the actualization of the Unitarian Universalist ideals into the nooks and crannies of our daily lives, they will never seem substantial. If our UU ideals never seem substantial in the lives of our congregants, those same ideals will never take root in the actions of our congregations. If our ideals never take root in the actions of our congregations, they will never be able to transform our world into the just, sustainable, and life affirming vision of which we dream.

We set forth very high ideals for our congregations, we leave people with the assumption that they must somehow act upon these ideals in their own lives, and then we provide little formal guidance or support about how they may be able to do that. We instead focus on our plurality of theological beliefs, or upon our corporate and individual speaking out through projects of social justice.

I am certain that this disconnect is apparent to much of our ministry, as I have heard it addressed from the pulpits of several different congregations. However, as more and more of the members and friends of our congregations connect with our churches in ways other than the Sunday morning worship (affinity groups, independent affiliate organizations, small group ministries), using the pulpit to bring the seven principles directly into peoples lives has never been very effective.

In looking for another way to address this disconnect between our modern Unitarian Universalism and this traditional responsibility of a religious faith, I found myself encountering another trend within

Unitarian Universalism, one that provides a clue as to how some UUs are addressing this disconnect within their own lives.

Rev. James Ishmael Ford, in an article in the online magazine *Buddhadharma* is quoted as saying that Unitarian Universalists who are exploring and self identifying as Buddhists may be "the largest convert Buddhist grouping in the country right now." (Boyce) The article describes that there are more than 125 separate Buddhist practice groups affiliated with Unitarian Universalist congregations.

The recent UUA Commission on Appraisal report, Engaging our Theological Diversity implies that the reason that many within our congregations are turning "outward" towards other religious traditions, including Buddhism, is that they are seeking more defined metaphors than are available within Unitarian Universalism. (UUA 29) I, however, believe it is for another, more fundamental reason. The attraction these faiths have for many in our pews is that they provide practical guidance for how to live a just, ethical, and affirming life.

This may be truer of western Buddhism than it is of many other traditions, which in part accounts for the rise in self identified "UU Buddhists" within our congregations. While many are seeking a spiritual practice, such meditation practices as exist in Buddhism do not require a conversion to practice. One does not become a Buddhist by the practice alone. It is rather, through the acceptance of the precepts in a formal ceremony of Jukai that one truly embraces Buddhism. (Maezumi 175)

A part of the explanation for this growing trend of Buddhism within Unitarian Universalism is the need to find a way to actualize the Unitarian Universalist ideals, expressed in the seven principles, in our individual and daily lives. Within this growing movement in our faith lies a lesson for our faith as a whole. Unless we realize and embrace the need to make our ideals practical in our lives, our congregations may continue to serve as a revolving door for many on a spiritual quest. No one knows how many have explored Unitarian Universalism only to leave our congregations looking for a more practical application of their faith.

Those who have stayed and found a way to combine their Unitarian Universalism with another tradition that provided such a practical practice of ethics often stay for reasons of community and justice. Steve Silverberg of the Eno River Buddhist Community in Durham, North Carolina, expressed it this way:

> *"I sense that UU Buddhist groups will often get to a point where they will find it necessary to consider taking responsibility for creating a form of Buddhist practice that more fully reflects our deepest values as UUs. Much of Buddhism resonates strongly with these values. However, many Buddhist traditions seem insufficiently conscious about issues such as religious authority, the importance of individual autonomy, the significance of ritual, the role of women, etc." (Trumbore)*

Since much of the seven principles can be understood in terms of community and justice, it could be said that UU Buddhists remain connected with the ideals and purposes of our liberal religious movement, but have sought a practice of those ideals from outside because they could not find one within.

How might a UU Buddhist find, within the Buddhist precepts, a way to live the ideals reflected within the seven principles in the daily conduct of life? I'm using the version of the Buddhist precepts that is presented by Diane Eshin Rizzetto in her book Waking Up to What You Do. This is a form of the precepts used within an active Zen community, and I chose them for three reasons. First, Zen is the most common form of Buddhism that finds itself expressed within a UU framework. Second, this version of the precepts is expressed in terms of goals to be achieved and not in terms of commandments to be obeyed, something many of those who come to Unitarian Universalism are seeking to evade. Indeed, even when expressed as commandments, the Buddhist precepts are different from the normal Christian conception of the Ten Commandments in that not living up to them is a challenge for the future and should not be a cause for guilt or shame. The third and most practical reason for choosing this expression of the Buddhist precepts is their smaller number, eight instead of sixteen or more. The monastic versions of the precepts can run to even hundreds (though, notably, had more for women than for men). Each school often has not only a different number of precepts, but they are also varying in their language and expression.

In short, in my look at the different forms of the precepts I found the version promulgated by Rizzetto to be significantly in line with a Unitarian Universalist mentality. They are expressed as:

> *I take up the way of speaking truthfully.*
> *I take up the way of speaking of others with openness*
> *   and possibility.*
> *I take up the way of meeting others on equal ground.*
> *I take up the way of cultivating a clear mind.*
> *I take up the way of taking only what is freely given and*
> *   giving freely of all that I can.*
> *I take up the way of engaging in sexual intimacy respect-*
> *   fully and with an open heart.*
> *I take up the way of letting go of anger.*
> *I take up the way of supporting life. (Rizetto 18)*

Much of the following reflection on the principles and the precepts has been as a part of my beginning zazen practice of meditation.

I take up the way of speaking truthfully

On a first read, this might be one of the less obvious precepts to relate to the seven principles, simply because of its regular applicability to daily life. Yet, at least two of our principles depend greatly for their authority and validity that we take up the way of speaking truthfully.

Those principles are "A free and responsible search for truth and meaning" and "Justice, equity, and compassion in human relations."

In order to search for truth, we must be in the practice of recognizing, expressing, and comparing truth. In order for a search for meaning to have validity, it must be an honest search. If we are unable to be truthful about who we are, what our needs and desires are, or why we choose to do the things we do, then a search for truth and meaning will not be free or responsible.

It is not only the practice of speaking truthfully that is important, but also the perception that we are people who have a practice of speaking truthfully. If we are not perceived as truthful, then there will never be any validity to our actions in the world in which we seek to promote "justice, equity, and compassion in human relations." As a religious movement, we are small in number compared to the larger population, no matter what figures you use. Yet, we are often able to have an effect many times what our numbers would imply, both as an association and as individuals doing social witness, social action, and social justice work. I believe the reason for this is that we are authentically engaged with the issues, and that we speak and witness about those issues from a stance of truthfulness.

I take up the way of speaking of others with openness and possibility

Of all of the precepts, this one might have the broadest range in applicability within UU ideals reflected in the seven principles.

In a world that is so often full of ugliness and evil, it would be easy to speak of and think of humanity as a whole in a very harsh light. In rejecting the doctrine of Original Sin, both the Unitarians and the Universalists early in their history chose instead to accept a view of humankind as inherently good, not inherently evil. In the throes of the abolitionist movement in the United States prior and during the American Civil War, both the Unitarians and the Universalists came to a more inclusive view of human worth and dignity, a movement that continues in our faith today.

Some have referred to the principle affirming the inherent worth and dignity of every person as naïve, including Rev. Dr. William Schulz in his essay "What Torture's Taught Me." (Schulz 13) In the harsh light of complete truthfulness, Rev. Schulz is undoubtedly right. However, in living this principle we are actually expressing a way of speaking of others with openness and possibility. To make the choice to see what is good and worthwhile in every person you meet is to meet them, and then speak of him or her with openness and possibility. A stance where the first and primary way we react to others is through the negative aspects of human nature shuts down the possibility of genuine encounter between us.

If there is any one lesson that is central to Unitarian Universalism, it is that there is more than one truth. In taking up this way of speaking of others, we commit ourselves to the truth that is more life-giving and affirming whenever we can. Spiritual growth, both as individuals and in religious community depends on this kind of open encounter full of possibilities.

I take up the way of meeting others on equal ground

In this radical view of equality, we often practice such encounter by democratic forms. More importantly, we practice this radical equality by respecting those who disagree with us. The "right of conscience" means that our equal ground does not have to be, and perhaps should not be the same ground. It is easy to meet with those who always agree with you. This practice would help us to better live up to the ideal of the "right of conscience" than we currently are as Unitarian Universalists, as we seek to find ways to welcome those of political perspectives different from the "common ground" of many Unitarian Universalists.

As we speak of and encounter others with openness and possibility, we also must view ourselves with the same openness and possibility in order to encounter them on an equal footing. This precept is a double-edged sword, for it challenges us neither to place ourselves below others, nor to raise ourselves above ourselves. It is a radical view of equality that is not equality before the law, but equality before life. It is a practical application in life of directly experiencing "the inherent worth and dignity of every person," and a way to practice "the right of conscience and the use of the democratic process in our congregations an in society at large."

The true practice of affirming another person's inherent worth and dignity is to affirm that worth and dignity not in theory, but in practice through daily encounter. All of the protests for equal rights mean little if we are unable to encounter on an equal footing those on whose behalf we are protesting. Without this practice within our lives, much of social justice and action on the issue of equal rights could be viewed as a form of paternalism.

I take up the way of cultivating a clear mind

Traditionally, this precept is phrased "I take up the way of not using alcohol." Many interpret it to include other mind-altering substances. In today's world, that would mean not only drugs, but also excessive use of video games, the internet, gambling, and many other types of addictive behavior. While often thought of as personal vices, each of these types of behavior has broad ranging effects upon all of those who we are in relationship with.

The Rizzetto version of this precept is differently phrased than many other Buddhist versions of the precepts. Yet it is rephrased in a way that gives the concept greater validity for Unitarian Universalists. Often, we UUs neglect the part of the "interdependent web" that reminds us we are part of that web, as well, and that to respect the whole we must respect ourselves. Such addictive behavior is often a sign of disrespect for ourselves—for our own inherent worth and dignity. We cannot respect others if we cannot first find respect for our own place in the interdependent web.

***

I take up the way of taking only what is freely given and giving freely of all that I can

Like a previous precept, this one also has broad applicability in how we live the ideals represented by the seven principles. It serves as a motivation towards conservation as well as a motivation towards charitable and justice-making works. However, for the purposes of this study, we will reflect on it only in relation to "the goal of world community with peace, liberty, and justice for all."

Our world is crowded and growing more so every day. This precept has in other versions of the precepts been phrased as "not stealing," and with each passing year the number of people on this world make that a greater and greater imperative. Like all of the precepts, just like all of the seven principles, this one is impossible to achieve in its perfection. Yet, it is in the attempt to take only what is freely given, and then to give freely of all you can that we have any hope of achieving a world founded in peace, liberty, and justice.

This precept more than any other, if practiced to the best of our ability by a growing number of people, could create a just world for the future. This precept does not just apply to money, but to time, to space, to resources, and to life itself. It means to take the time that I need for myself when I have the opportunity, but then to give of my time the best that I can. It means to use the resources of this planet responsibly in my daily life. It means to share this world in a way that meets others on equal ground. Most importantly, it calls each of us to work for the world that we dream of with each waking moment of our lives.

I take up the way of engaging in sexual intimacy respectfully and with an open heart

One thing that religions have understood since the dawn of human remembrance is that there is great power in sex. It is a power to heal, and it is a power to wound. It is a power to build relationship, and it is a power to rip relationship apart. In fear of the power within this aspect of our nature, many religions, including some schools of Buddhism, have forbidden it from the ordained, and sought to limit it in the laity.

Yet the power of sex is beyond that kind of control, and in seeking to control it in this way, we can allow the sexual urge to control us. To view this precept from a vantage of learning and committing to engage in the power of sex through respect and openness is the only responsible way to respect our own inherent worth and dignity. It is also the only way to respect the power inherent in sex within the interdependent web of all existence.

Though it could be considered part of "meeting others on equal ground" or "taking only what is freely given," the importance of sex in building and maintaining relationship, loving partnership, and procreation is signified by a separate precept. It also signifies how it can also be one of the greatest dangers to living a just, affirming, and sustaining life.

Simply put, without a responsible way to engage with this power, we cannot recognize the inherent worth and dignity of others, or respect the place of others or ourselves in the interdependent web of all existence. Committing to this precept is to put into practice that respect in your own life, for yourself, for others, and for one of the most power-filled forces within human existence.

I take up the way of letting go of anger

Also conceivably covered in the spirit of several of the other precepts, the recognition of the need for a specific precept to address anger recognizes the power of this particular emotion over human life and behavior. This precept does not say that we shall not experience anger, nor does it say we should suppress anger. It speaks instead of choosing not to hold on to it, of choosing not to nurture it, of choosing to let it go.

When anger motivates us to work to end an injustice in the world, it is a positive thing. Yet, when we hold onto anger, it can lead us into a betrayal of every one of the seven principles. By learning to let go of our anger, we live our principles in our daily lives.

By letting go of anger, we allow ourselves to let go of a focus on the negative aspects of humanity that can prevent our seeing the inherent worth and dignity in each of us. By letting go of anger, we are able to engage each other with justice, equity, and compassion. By letting go of our anger we find acceptance of others in our own hearts, and find our own acceptance in theirs. By letting go of anger, we are not locked into positions that prevent our search for truth and meaning. By letting go of anger, we can engage each other in equitable processes that allow all voices to be not only heard, but listened to. By letting go of anger, we have a chance at peace, a chance at liberty, and a chance at justice. By letting go of anger, we can find something much greater … respect. We find respect for ourselves, and for all those with whom we share the web of existence. By letting go of anger, we prevent hatred. By letting go of anger, we lessen shame.

I take up the way of supporting life

The key to this practice within daily life is found not in this wording of the precept, but actually in the wording of the principle: respect. To have and show a continuing respect for life, all life, is to support life. To have the respect necessary to support life is to insure that you take no more than you need, and that you allow for the replenishment of what it is that you take. However, it is more than this. When we take life, we are then indebted to life. Therefore, by the very nature of how we need to consume life to sustain life, we are then responsible to use the life that is sustained in ways that are positive and productive in the world.

This precept allows us to live our principles by requiring us to respect the interdependent web; to recognize how connected we are not just to other human beings (as in the metaphor of Indra's Web) but also with every other living and non-living part of this universe. The interdependent web is not something within the universe; it is the universe. We are called and required to support that web, to support the universe. Can there be a more divine calling than this?

✼✼✼

Each of these precepts represents a way to live our Unitarian Universalist principles within our daily lives. Each of these precepts is not a commandment that will bring shame, but a challenge that will bring fulfillment. Each of these precepts represents, to me, what it truly means to be a Unitarian Universalist.

Providing a system that actualizes these principles in our daily lives is the first step in saving the world. It really is that profound, and so long as Unitarian Universalism continues to operate without being intentional about how we live our daily lives, we will never succeed in our vision for the world.

Such a system does not have to be the one described by the Buddhist precepts, but it does need to be something like them. The beauty of basing such a system of personal ethics upon the Buddhist precepts is that they have a 2,500 year old history, a large and growing number of our congregants have already adopted them ahead of us, and they are phrased as goals to be achieved, not commandments that cause shame. They also can be adopted as an ethical system regardless of whether or not they are accompanied by a practice of mediation or an acceptance of the cosmology of Buddhism.

Most importantly, each of the precepts reflects the deepest aspects of our own ideals, reflected in the seven principles. Through them, or a system like them, we can remake our world.

Henry Nelson Wieman and his Influence on My Theology

Tracy Springberry
Student

Written for Process Theology Class

I have always struggled with faith. What do I have faith in? What is solid and real and worth valuing? What gives hope when all seems hopeless? Raised by secular academics, I learned that what you can trust is yourself, and that you, yourself, are ultimately responsible for performance, success, and justice. Consumerist/late capitalist society reinforced this message—each person is completely responsible for his or her own economic and social well-being and how you look and what you buy will save oneself, our families and our communities. Unitarian Universalism as a religious tradition also reinforces this belief. In my church the motto is "What You Do Matters." Salvation, our minister preaches, is achieved by the integrity of one's own character or being. Certainly, other possibilities for faith are alluded to in all these cultures and traditions, but the central feature is faith in individuals' abilities to do the right thing.

I have found the weight of this responsibility terrifying and depressing. If what I can have faith in is my own ability to perform, then I know both the world and myself are doomed. I simply cannot do all that has to be done; what I can do, I cannot do perfectly. My lifelong tendency to believe that I am not good enough and that my not "good enoughness" matters deeply is not a surprising conclusion when I learned that all I can trust is myself. If my abilities are the ultimate Good, than what I do matters tremendously, and it matters much more than I can deliver.

Many people have crises about faith. While I clearly have not found the faith offered by my childhood to be particularly sustaining, my religious crises have been ones of values and ethics. They have been moral crises. This makes sense. If the ultimate faith is in myself then the way I behave makes a huge difference. So I worry about the correct way to be in the world. I want to know if the choices I make are ensuring the flourishing of my family, community and self.

I was raised by academics and am myself highly educated. What I was trained to do, and what seems as natural as breathing, is to think rationally. I mull the evidence. What I have faith in and what guides my moral choices cannot contradict the scientific evidence, cannot contradict what we know of history and of psychology, anthropology and sociology, and cannot contradict my experience. I doubt I will make a leap and find sustenance in a personal God who is beyond history and nature. Still experiential evidence demonstrates that life is more mysterious and interesting than we can rationally understand: there is synchronicity, moments of grace, falling in love, call to vocation, the intensity of birth and death. My heart, mind, and spirit call me to have faith in and be guided by something beyond myself.

Enter Henry Nelson Wieman

Henry Nelson Wieman was an influential liberal theologian in the middle part of this century. He taught at the Divinity School at the University of Chicago beginning in 1927 and published 16 books and many articles—two of the most well known are Source of Human Good, published in 1946, and Man's Ultimate Commitment, published in 1958. Wieman was first and foremost an empirical theologian. In Source of

Human Good, Wieman says "nothing can happen if it does not happen." (8) He was also initially influenced by Alfred Whitehead's speculative metaphysics.

Henry Nelson Wieman expressed the fundamental question of his intellectual quest this way:

> *"What operates in human life with such character and power that it will transform men and women as they cannot transform themselves, save them from evil and lead them to the best that human life can ever reach, provided they meet the required conditions?" (Southworth 3)*

His question asks, "What can we have faith in? What can guide our behavior?" Wieman lays out his answer to this question in the Source of Human Good. He begins by asking what is actually "good" and creates "good." He rejects value as objects, satisfaction, quality and human control. While Wieman argues that each of these can be "good," they are meaningless to guide our behavior. For example, if we use satisfaction of human needs as a guide for deciding what is good we can be confused when what satisfies changes or when we must sort out differing needs between people. For Wieman finding an understanding for what was "good" that could guide behavior was critical. In this era of Wieman's work, he was struggling with World War II and the undeniable evidence that as a species we had the capacity to destroy on a massive scale. "The life and death of increasing millions hang on our discovery of a universal principle that can guide us in choosing good that is common to all" (Source 12)."

Wieman decided that the best way to solve the problem of what is "good" was to correlate good with qualitative meaning. This is rich meaning that reverberates in our lives and adds layers of understanding and depth to the world. "Good increases as qualitative meaning increases." (Source 19) But, he says, qualitative meaning is not the ultimate good; the ultimate good is what makes qualitative meaning possible.

This is creativity or the "creative event."

The creative event, according to Wieman, is the reorganization of a person to have new, deeper meanings in relationship with others and the world. In doing so, the person appreciates the quality of life in richer ways. The creative event is the same as personal and cultural transformation. He calls the creative event or creative good "absolute good" and he means the creative good is always good no matter the time or place or person or race or class. It is changeless. Qualitative meaning is "created good." The actual structure of qualitative meaning, what has been created through the creative event, can become demonic or evil.

In Source of Human Good, Wieman describes four sub-events to the creative event and all must be present for the creative event to have happened:

> *emerging awareness of qualitative meaning derived from other people through communication;"*
>
> *integrating these new meanings into self;*
>
> *expanding and appreciating the world by enlarging its meaning; and*
>
> *widening and deepening community and increased interrelatedness. (58)*

Wieman argues that human beings need to conduct their lives to encourage the creative event, but that we cannot control the creative event or guide it to our own outcome. "The creative event cannot be used to shape the world closer to the heart's desire because it transforms the heart's desire so that one wants something very different from what one desired in the beginning." (57). Throughout the Source of Human Good, Wieman gives several examples of the ways that people can be open to creative events in their own lives. People can 1) give the self to be transformation; 2) spend time in solitude; 3) actively worship; 4) pray; 5) increase sensitivity to the world; and 6) have long-standing association with one another in small groups. Wieman also has suggestions for cultural change to release creative events. They are to 1) modify institutional structures so people can participate in creative interchange; 2) awaken initiative and responsibility of people in local situations; and 3) propagate religious faith.

Wieman's Influence on my Theology

Not long after I first read Wieman, I had a profound experience of the healing power of a faith that was beyond myself, a faith in Wieman's creative event. I had had a difficult interaction with my father. We have a distant and rocky relationship; one I've struggled to make peace with. In this instance, my father, who lives in the same town and works at the same university as I do, choose not to attend either of the readings of my just- released book. I was angry and hurt and at a loss as to how to respond. After years of counseling, I felt I should know how to respond. Also, I felt, since I believed that ultimate faith rested in myself, how I responded mattered very much. By my actions, I could respond in a way that would bring love and healing to the world or in a way that would not. By my actions, I could bring love and healing into the relationship.

Then, I remembered, at a critical moment, Wieman said we cannot control the outcome of a creative event. We cannot make the creative event happen. We can simply be present and open to it happening. The most beautiful delicious feeling of clarity and peace washed over me. I knew suddenly I did not have the power to transform the relationship with my father—not now, not ever. All I could do was be open to transformation, and communicate with myself, him and others to encourage the first step of the creative process. I could say, "I was hurt." That was my responsibility.

I experienced transformation in that moment of realization. I felt both peace and a new way of looking at the world. I felt less tangled with anxiety and could be more open to others. I could only do as much as I could do, and I could not fix it, that was okay, that was the responsibility of the creative element of the universe. I had found something I could have faith in that did not ask me to set aside my scientific understanding of the world. Also this discovery saved me from ultimate responsibility for every hurtful, difficult, evil situation. It gave me ways to take personal responsibility while having faith that something more than me also had a role in changing myself and others toward greater good.

PART TWO:

THE SERMONS

Roads: Taken and Not

Stephen Atkinson, MDiv '07

The Unitarian Fellowship of Fredericton, NB, Canada

May 12, 2006

A teenager peers across the cafeteria for the umpteenth time to catch a glimpse of the dark-eyed girl that just joined his Physics class. She's new to the school and probably doesn't have a date for the prom, but he's always been shy. He looks down again at his boring lunch, but then some new gear inside him drives him all the way across the room to interrupt her conversation and invite her to the dance. Shortly after, but only when he's almost to the Library, does he truly get that she said yes, and he thinks, "Maybe I'm not shy after all."

A nurse pops into the liquor store to pick up some wine after a long shift. As she approaches the check-out, she sees the man who left her two years ago, saying, of all crazy things, that she drinks too much. She starts to hide the bottle behind her back, but he finishes paying and leaves without seeing her. She suddenly finds herself at the counter, but now with a 40 ouncer of J&B instead of wine. Her body feels as though it's falling through clouds and gaining speed, but her hands make the payment. She thinks, "This'll go perfectly with those little pills I'm sampling from the pharmacy cart." She can't wait to get home.

A woman is on a flight to Europe after a visit home to her small city in the Midwest for her twentieth high school reunion. She strikes up a conversation with the college student sitting beside her. He is bucking the trend among his classmates and going to Paris for Spring Break instead of Pensacola. She tells him about how she waited tables for a year in Germany after college, and now writes policy for the World Health Organization in Geneva. She smiles, noticing a tiny light flick on in his eyes as he starts to consider a whole new world of possibility.

These stories mark points on the road of each character in them. The teenager takes a chance he'd normally avoid, and it just might change his character. The nurse refuses to face what is obvious to those around her; unlike her ex-boyfriend, she fails to make a healthy decision. The woman on the plane made an early choice that helped her make a difference in the world; her satisfaction prompts her to plant a seed in the mind of someone she identifies with. What will happen to the seed we don't know.

When I first talked about writing this sermon, several people asked if I'd be using the Robert Frost poem that so many of us associate with the topic of roads taken and decisions made. "The road less traveled" has become a famous phrase, although it's not a direct quote from the poem. It is a wonderful image of choice and individuality, and has been especially powerful for many of us Unitarian Universalists; but it raises a question. To me, readers overemphasize the allure of the 'less traveled road,' especially considering Frost also says that it is only slightly less worn than the other route. Also, I fear Frost overstates himself, claiming that his choice makes "all the difference." My problem with this is that it diminishes the value of taking the well-worn road, which many of us choose to do or must do; it is not for anyone to assume that this is a lesser choice; and surely, if the poem is about choice, than whatever we choose makes a difference, no choice making all the difference. It's important to refer to it in our service today, but in itself it is not the last word on this subject.

As some of you may recall, I happen to love maps. Remember, at my first sermon as an intern here last summer, how I brought out a map to show the whole congregation where I come from? There's a personal awareness exercise that probably most of us have done and found useful at some point in our lives. We draw a straight line across a page and mark on it the big moments in our lives: events that have happened, or decisions we've made. When I began to think about decisions, about 'roads: taken and not', I started to picture such an exercise in which we also map out some of the alternate paths our lives could have taken, if we had… well, fill in the blank. Chosen a different university? Not turned down an invitation? Taken dance lessons? Those are all decisions I faced at some point in the past that I now realize have had life-long implications.

Just like the lines on the palms of our hands, a true life-line is never straight. Instead, a fully fleshed out life looks more like a winding and splitting path. Many of our maps would look pretty loopy: omigoodness, I've made that old mistake again! What I wouldn't give to make a brand new mistake! Our drawings would look more like the trail we make when we're lost in the woods, and, only on the third pass by an odd-shaped tree, realize that we're going in circles! And none of us have just one stream of life at any time. We have families, careers, favorite pastimes; we have the church. We have parallel goals, or conflicting ones; multiple demands drawing us on.

And, unlike the exercise which intentionally focuses our eyes on progress we've made, an accurate map would make us think also about parts of ourselves that we left behind. Although in theory, it's helpful to see life as moving us inexorably forward towards some future fulfillment, life doesn't often feel that way. Truer maps would reveal our regrets and unfulfilled hopes as dead end offshoots of the main path; directions we had hoped to go, but which just ended. Perhaps we injured a knee, or a heart. Or talked ourselves out of an option that seemed impractical. Or let a whim end a friendship. Such maps would uncover pain that we like to think is behind us or dreams that we thought we'd given up. The pay-off of maps like these is that they point us toward what we might really need or want to do next.

Let's not forget that some of our maps seem at times to be infuriating mazes or wicked puzzles set out for us to solve. Carl Jung talks about the Shadow within each personality that may have its own version of our path. The Shadow is a part of us denied or suppressed and can be, but is not always destructive. It can contain power and energy not available through our conscious will. Our Shadow road can threaten to divert us entirely, but it also might lead us to buried treasure hidden inside.

A deeply honest map would show the dotted lines of what I'll call nightmare roads; these are routes we somehow escaped but may not be fully safe from. An example comes from addiction theory, which holds that the addictive process continues to trace a vestigial path even once recovery is underway. Those who relapse can go frighteningly quickly from one little slip to the old pattern that was the problem before and, the scary part, even further down to where they would have been if they'd not been in recovery at all. A force like addiction can trace a nightmare road beside our life line, but knowing this underscores the presence of the dormant disease, the need to fully commit to recovery and the importance of gratitude for what blesses and saves us. Other such traumas can linger on like a dark temptation: today, I feel like just staying in and shutting all my blinds for a whole day like I used to when I was depressed. It seems so attractive right now, but ... no, that really stopped working long ago, and I've got those notes to write to last Sunday's visitors. Better get up!

This subject of roads and life-lines brings us to a fate/freedom dichotomy. The mainstream thinking in Unitarian Universalism holds that we are simply free: many, but not all of us have rejected the idea that a supernatural power exerts influence on us or our lives, whether we label such power 'Fate' in the Classical sense, or use the religious concept of God. In one way, this idea is truly freeing, handing us the reins of our own wagons to direct towards any point on the horizon that we feel is right. But, in another sense, we are also fated to be free; this is a phrase from James Luther Adams, the most prominent Unitarian theologian of the Twentieth Century. He, like the Existentialists, talks of how human beings are unavoidably free; even when we don't want to, we must take responsibility for what we do. A decision avoided is a decision made. An act denied is no less a part of our history.

While I was in university, the comedian, Flip Wilson, had the funniest show on television; his most famous character was Geraldine, who'd come home to find her husband unhappy that she had spent more money shopping. Geraldine's famous line was, "The devil made me buy this dress!" Funny as Flip Wilson was, that excuse is meaningless in our Unitarian Universalist world, and I'm glad it is—sort of.

I say 'sort of' because in my mind and heart and soul, it's unsatisfying to think that every moment of life is a product of conscious choice, or unconscious choice, for that matter. Some people boil down the idea of fate to genetic and environmental determination or the workings of the unconscious mind. It's not that I don't see an awesome power in these realities, or find fascinating the mysteries beyond number in the natural world that we have yet to solve; I just don't find complete nourishment from these ideas. I suppose there's a calculable probability for the time when a friend from seminary was lost in the Chicago subway system at rush hour, and just happened upon the one person from our school that was coming home from his job way out in the suburbs through that exact station at that very moment. She thought of it as chance or luck, while I want to see grace at work in such coincidences: the gentle, persistent suggestions of grace that bend our attention ever so little at the exact moment to turn at the perfect angle towards what guides us to our truest home.

And, speaking of such coincidences, I chose our first reading from a book of Rilke poetry I recently bought. I happened to ask a member of the Intern Committee if he would conduct the service today, meaning that he would read this poem for us. He was delighted to say yes because he already knew it by heart! The senior minister here at First Unitarian Church of Dallas, Dr. Laurel Hallman, was introduced to this poem by her mentor twenty years ago; he told her to memorize and meditate upon it, and it helped her decide to accept the call to this church. She uses this poem in her spirituality program, Living By Heart, which my friend is now leading in the church. Now what are the chances of that, I ask you?

I want to tell you another story like those that I opened with today, but this time it's a true one. There is a 16 year old youth at First Dallas who has given me permission to say a bit about him this evening. Our Religious Education leaders, as well as the youth, have seen over the years that this young man leads by quiet example. For instance, he decided to grow his hair to the waist, and I'm told it was gorgeous, thick hair most women would covet; then he had it cut off and donated to Locks of Love, the organization that makes wigs for people with cancer. His sister joined him in doing this, as have a number of the youth in our church, some growing and donating their hair more than once. This boy has struggled with a rare neurological condition for almost a year; he's been admitted to the hospital several times, lost school time and been separated from friends. He's a brainy kid, and sees the irony that it's his brain that's a threat to him. In the homily that he has sent us to be read on Youth Sunday, he writes,

> *"It is with great clarity that I am developing an essential understanding that life isn't always fair, it is how we work with what we are given that teaches us how to live. Clearly, without the heart, the brain has nothing to rely on.... The plans that we make in life aren't always the direction we continue on. Sometimes life shows us that we have a bigger plan, a greater journey and we become significantly stronger within this new path."*

Sixteen years old.

The roads we are on are part of "a bigger plan, a greater journey." Whoever or whatever is the mapmaker; whether the route resembles a path in the woods or a trail through the jungle, an arrow-straight highway, a confusing maze or an ancient map to buried treasure. Whatever the road, something moves us onward, which brings us back to Rilke. Let's hear it again.

My eyes already touch the sunny hill,
going far ahead of the road I have begun.
So we are grasped by what we cannot grasp;
it has its inner light, even from a distance—
and changes us, even if we do not reach it,
into something else, which hardly sensing it, we already
     are;
a gesture waves us on, answering our own wave . . .
but what we feel is the wind in our faces.

I will offer you one of many possible readings of this poem, just one interpretation. For each of us something acts as our sunny hill, our own greatest hope that we see far ahead of us; it orients our motion. We have only an idea of what it is on that horizon. We cannot know it before being there, but something draws us on even though we can't know its reality. The direction we aim in; the desire to move towards it; the journey itself changes us, but the inner light on that distant hill acts upon us as sunlight upon a seed. Some part of us that already exists hidden within starts to form and gather power. And this happens even if we do not reach the end because it is aiming for the goal itself, the movement itself which feeds the transformation. In our depths, we yearn for the light far ahead, and something in us waves in honor of it; and that for which we long beckons back to us, honoring our desire. But, the journey is of the heart and soul. What we immediately encounter is only what is right up against us where we actually are or coming at us as a kind of resistance like a headwind. Despite our orientation forward, this wind, these forces affect our path, whether they come from within or whether they are obstacles put in our way. This is the journey of a life.

I will leave you with a final image. When we watch on film a race, like the marathon, we are shown camera positions from different points of view, yet when we run our own race, we are stuck in the view to which our tired, sweating bodies constrain us. Every so often, we must stop and place ourselves in the position of the sharp-eyed eagle flying high above; from there we see the whole route: where we are, where we've been and what is the lay of the land. We can judge whether we're still interested in the race, or whether that path off to the left just around the corner looks more alluring. And, from up there, we get a clearer view of that distant, sunny hill that holds such fascination and grants us our second wind.

Let us remember to take moments to inhabit the eagle, to gaze down upon the whole road. To get oriented, and re-oriented, and re-oriented again. The horizon is far away, and the road itself is the goal.

May it be so.

Within These Four Walls

Eliza Galaher, MDiv '07

Presented before the Ministerial Fellowship Committee

December 4, 2006

Living in New York City in my twenties, there were moments when I'd be walking down the street, or riding in the subway, when suddenly, a line of a poem would come into my head, and then, like cars of a train themselves, line after line would start tumbling forward, and, if I didn't have pen and paper, I would have to scurry to repeat and remember the accumulating lines, careful to keep them all within me until I got home—or got somewhere—to write them all down. In those moments of composing, I had to speak the words, I had to conduct the lines coming forth, however subtly, as traffic passed and passersby carried on their own conversations. And if others caught a glance of me in my own incantation, whatever they may have thought of me, it didn't matter. I was on my way to a new poem.

These days, and for many years really, those lines don't descend upon me like they did back in New York. Rarely am I suddenly startled by the beauty of that first phrase rushing into or up from within me. These days, knowing a paper is due, or a church newsletter article, or a prayer, I mostly sit and wait. And the words are willing, and they come, and I am still blessed with this love of language and what it can do. But I will admit, I miss those days, back in New York, feeling almost struck, often sent hopefully searching for a pen some other pedestrian or train rider must have dropped ahead of me—searching for a napkin, a menu, something to write on. I admit, with those days gone, to call myself a poet no longer feels so natural. For whatever reason, that pace, that rhythm, that meter have traded themselves in for a slower, longer form of writing, and it is that newer form that opens itself here now.

What created that shift? What drew the muse away from delivering me a line, a line break, a next line, an internal rhyme? I can't say for certain. But suddenly that muse was gone. Or, more likely, it's not so much that she left, but that perhaps she felt communication needed improvement—new forms, new styles, new ears and eyes. And so, after living as a poet finding poems in the smells of dumpsters and the sounds of tracks being rattled below my pedestrian feet, I found myself slowly letting go … and waiting. Here I am. Here are the words, slower; here are the lines, longer; with breaks ruled by margins more than by breath.

What new margins, what new rhythms or rules have you found yourself living within? Maybe it is walking instead of running, maybe it is retirement instead of work. Maybe it is new parenthood filling the time for yourself you couldn't see losing, or maybe it is a relationship moving from the rush of romance to the quiet gratitude of deep, long-running love. Whatever shifts come our way, how do we relate to them, work with them? The other day, I heard a favorite singer/songwriter of mine being interviewed on the radio. I'd first discovered her in New York, when she was just breaking through. These days, she lives in Texas, and has just come out of a three-year writing drought. On the radio, she'd played a new song, with the refrain, "I'll die within these four walls." When the song was over, the interviewer responded, "that pulls at my heart strings … I can't tell if it's resignation? Or contentment?" to which the singer responded, "Both, both."

To find our four walls, and to live within them, can sound stifling to a religious community that demands that revelation is not sealed, that affirms and promotes a free and responsible search for truth and meaning. It can sound like the clicking shut of a prison door. But in my seminary studies, I have been reminded of my need to claim, rather than disdain the walls of my own humanity. One of the first books I picked up in my first year of seminary was Augustine's Confessions. I remember the struggle I experienced as a reader, sifting through Augustine's fight to find peace within himself as he worked through torn desires of body and soul. He did eventually find a solution, a surrender really, in the moment he turned to the Bible and fell upon the passage that read, in part, "Make not provision for the flesh …".

Reading that passage, Augustine discovered a peace that until that time had eluded him. But while this was originally a personal solution in the life of this one man, because of his tremendous influence on Christian theology, it has become, in its ideals and in its pedagogy, a theological standard as well. But the standard is one of dichotomy rather than unity. In my experience, it makes for a disembodied theology, ultimately detrimental to wholeness. For it is actually when trying to crawl out of our own skin—when we try to leave the four walls of our very humanity—that we do harm to ourselves. As a young runner, I used to run as if trying to run away from my body. But there came a time when, rather than seeing my body as the cause of my troubles, I saw instead that it—that is, me—was sticking with me, with an almost heart-breaking loyalty.

I'll die within these four walls. That being true, let me truly live within these four walls. Within these four walls, I will live and grow and change, and age. Scribbles become poems become sermons. Crawling becomes walking becomes running becomes walking again. Within these four walls, we will change, and yet remain the same. Within these four walls, we will continually live out a free and responsible search for truth and meaning.

I'm reminded of a story about Universalist religious educator, Angus MacLean. Having grown up with orthodox understandings of God and religion, MacLean found himself, upon leaving orthodoxy behind, living for a time in a sad void of meaning making. Then, one day, as a biographer notes, "while contemplating a patch of swampy ground, [MacLean] suddenly perceived it as a profound creative source: 'What a marvelous ooze,' I said—and I had my God again!" Whether it is ooze or the muse that brings us back to the sacred, it brings us back in ever-changing ways, and it does so within the walls of our ever-changing selves.

As we change and grow and age and slow, may we listen and look. May we be open to all that life brings to us, and teaches us. And may we remember, as we do, to carry pen and paper. For you never know when or where you will be struck, and chances are there will very likely be something well worth writing down.

Amen.

Sisters and Brothers

Aaron McEmrys, MDiv '07

First Unitarian Society of Denver

September 17, 2006

My first big lesson on the meaning and power of brotherhood happened when I was ten years old or so. My two little sisters and I were standing at the bus stop waiting to go to school. Laura was about eight and Andrea, the baby, was six. It was a cold, rainy fall morning. We had just moved into a new neighborhood and this was our first time at this bus stop.

We were all nervous, which goes without saying, but also important to this story is the fact that we couldn't stand one another! Our house was kind of like a three-bedroom de-militarized zone, and I thought being trapped in the same family with them was about the cruelest fate anyone could have.

In fact, I walked my sisters to the bus stop under duress, after being sternly ordered to look after them by my mom. So I walked as far ahead of them as I could; pretending they weren't with me.

I was lounging against a streetlamp, trying to look cooler and more confident than I felt around all the new kids, when a group of older boys, you know the ones, every schoolyard has them—surrounded my sisters.

I did nothing. For one thing, I didn't want to get on the wrong side of the bullies right off the bat—that could make for a very long year.

And more importantly—I couldn't stand my sisters! But as I stood there motionless, in a crowd of other spectators, a heavy, sick feeling started to grow in my belly. One of the bullies knocked Andrea's books and school supplies out of her arms and onto the ground, and when she bent over to pick them up, he kicked them so they scattered all over. She was starting to cry, and it was if I could feel her shame, her fear, her impotent rage in my own body.

Before I knew it I was there, between her and the bullies. "Get away from my sister," I said, my voice not nearly as brave or threatening as I would have liked. The bullies sized me up and I could see that my worst fears were about to be realized. Then, out of the blue, my other sister Laura stepped up and said, "You leave my brother alone!"

We were saved by the school bus pulling up to the curb. We got on the bus, and never spoke of it again, at least not until adulthood. We went back to our accustomed squabbling without blinking, but deep down I think we all knew something important had happened. They were my sisters and I was their brother. Period.

Experiences like this one make up the foundation of my vision of what sisterhood is: what it feels like, what it means, and what it costs to honor it. This touches on a deeply spiritual question—"to whom are we related?"

We are inextricably interconnected in the web of life. And for me, the web of life is sacred. So while some of my relationships are closer than others, I believe that everybody is my brother, my sister. It's not a question of whether we are related, but whether we know we are related, and whether we honor that relationship. For me, the world is made up of sisters and brothers that I know—and sisters and brothers that are still strangers.

This idea is called the imago dei in theological parlance. It is the notion that all of us are made of the same sacred stuff, that we all bear the light of holiness simply because we are part of this vast and beautiful web of life. Some call this being made in the image of God. To see the imago dei in someone else is to recognize their sacred relationship to you and to the rest of creation.

One of the things that makes it hard to see ourselves as sisters and brothers is that such relationships can only exist where there is genuine equality. As liberation theologian Nancy Eisland writes,

> *"Such interdependence is not a possibility that can be willed from a position of power, but a necessary condition of life. This interdependence is the fact of both justice and survival. This kind of relationship embodies practical interdependence, not simply willing to be inter -related from a position of power, but depending on it from a position of need." (Eisland 103)*

Hard as it is to relate to one another like this in our own immediate relationships, it is exponentially more difficult in the wider world. We live in a society that is organized around who is included and who isn't. The list of the excluded is long and all too familiar to us.

What happens when society denies the humanity, the imago dei, of one group in particular? There are laws and social prescriptions to prevent or discourage intermarriage, even sex between members of this group. Many are routinely denied employment, housing, medical care and even access to public buildings. They are a group of people often forced to become dependant on the charity of others. Although there are many paths to membership in this group, poverty, malnutrition and violence are the most common pathways by far.

I'm talking about persons with disabilities. There are a lot of phrases I could use here: "differently-abled" is another widely accepted option these days, but I choose "persons with disabilities" because "it underscores the conviction that an individual's disability is just one of many personal characteristics, rather than being synonymous with that person's self." (Eisland 27)

"Persons with disabilities" is not a monolithic group. The category includes a huge range of mental and physical characteristics, embodied in individuals as unique as snowflakes. "Persons with disabilities are distinguished not because of our shared physical, psychological, or emotional traits, but because temporarily able-bodied persons single us out for different treatment." (Eisland 24)

George W. Bush helped persuade me to preach on this today. On August 29, 2006, the United Nations passed the first human rights convention of the 21st century. It is the UN Convention on the Rights of Persons with Disabilities, a convention designed to insure that the 650 million people living with disabilities in our world will be insured the same rights and opportunities as everyone else. The United States government has announced that we will not sign the treaty, and will not honor its provisions. Thanks for the motivation, George.

Roughly 43 million Americans live with disabilities, that's one out of every six people. (ADA p 329)

And I am one of them.

When I was sixteen I was run over by a car, leaving me paralyzed from the waist down. It has taken quite a few years, but my body has made an incredible recovery. Of course, I still live every day with a lot of pain. And although I am healthy at the moment, I live with the certain knowledge that I am always just one small accident away from living the rest of my life in a wheelchair. I can feel in excruciating detail various parts of my injured body wearing down, collapsing, falling apart. This is my life.

I have to share with you some of the fear and anxiety I feel about preaching this sermon today. I am new here. And I am one of your ministers. I thought long and hard about whether sharing this part of my story would make it harder for you to see me as a person and as a minister. I thought about whether it wouldn't be more "tactically" prudent to wait until "later" when you knew me a bit better.

But then I realized that that's what I have been doing for years. Living with the most central parts of myself hidden behind a veil. This denial of self is very common among people with disabilities. It is often driven by shaming we experience over and over in our social interactions, shaming which is inevitably internalized to some degree, like a parasite—

a shame, a rejection of self that we begin to believe is part of who we are.

On a personal level I just don't want to do that anymore. I want to be my whole self. But on another level I feel compelled to speak as a minister. I am called to speak the truth in love and to work for justice. I am called to be a voice not only for the immediate communities I serve, but for all the people whose voices are not heard. If I won't speak about this—who will?

So here I am, preaching the sermon I feel called to preach this week. What you make of it, and of me, is up to you. The stories I will share with you today are not confessionals. I have chosen to share personal stories that echo the stories many other people with disabilities have shared with me through the years.

In our society there are two primary images of people with disabilities, both of which deny the full humanity of our brothers and sisters with disabilities. I like to call the first image, "Tiny Tim." This is the image of people with disabilities as vulnerable, dependant, needing our help. They are objects of pity and compassion, but objects nonetheless. Think of the teary-eyed spectacle of Jerry Lewis's' annual Labor Day Telethons.

It is not hard to sympathize with people with disabilities, but it can be very hard to empathize—to really put ourselves in their place— because much of what persons with disabilities experience is so far outside the lived experiences of the able-bodied. I think this is one of the things at the root of the discomfort many able-bodied people experience around people with disabilities. People share feelings of awkwardness: wanting to act "normal" and "respectful," but not feeling sure of how to do that. People also share their feelings of guilt with me—guilt that they are currently able-bodied while another is not. People often tell me they feel ashamed of themselves for not knowing how to act, or when they catch themselves staring or averting their eyes or saying something insensitive. These feelings don't mean that we are bad people.

The fact that so many able-bodied people share feelings like this with me is not indicative of their individual shortcomings, but of a much wider and deeper spiritual ailment at work in our culture. The antidote for experiences and feelings like these lies in more relationship, for it is only through relationship that we can recognize the kinship between us.

I have been treated as a "Tiny Tim," especially when I was still in my wheelchair and looked less "normal." I will never forget the burning shame of having to ask someone to carry me up a flight of stairs, or into a bathroom stall that was too small for my chair. I can still feel the heat rise in my cheeks as I remember all the times I have caught people staring at me, or worse, referring to me as "my paraplegic friend, Aaron" when they didn't know I could overhear them.

Our society's second primary image of people with disabilities is what theologian Nancy Eisland calls the image of the "overcomer." The image of the overcomer is one in which people can conquer their dis-abilities through sheer will. Movies like "My Left Foot," "A Dangerous Mind," and "The Helen Keller Story" may make for moving stories, but they do not reflect the ordinary lives of persons with disabilities any more than watching Michael Jordan play basketball reflects what you or I can do on a basketball court if we try hard enough. But think about it—how many portrayals of persons with disabilities have you seen that are not of Tiny Tim's or Overcomers?

I learned quickly that playing the part of "overcomer" was more palatable to me, if also more exhausting. So instead of pity, I sought ad-miration. I pushed my body as far as it could go, often farther than was safe. Mountain climbing, fencing, tennis, soccer—isn't it incredible what Aaron can do with his paralyzed legs! But deep down I knew that people still weren't seeing the real me.

As my body healed, and began to look more "normal," I started trying to "pass" for "able-bodied," something not all of my kin with disabilities can do or would choose to do.

Years ago I was working as an actor for a theatre company in New York. It was my first "big" show and I was so proud and excited for the chance to prove myself. Here I was—after years of dreaming and hard work. Every morning I would walk into the rehearsal hall and revel in the dusty, vaguely paint-tinged smell of the theatre.

I was pretty nervous about the dancing. One of my legs is entirely paralyzed from the right knee down and the other is about half paralyzed—useable, but only in a very rudimentary way. I wore long pants every day so no one would see my leg brace.

One day, in the middle of one of those sweltering New York heat waves the air conditioner went down. It must've been 110 degrees in the rehearsal hall. I was dying in my long pants, but I wouldn't take them off.

We were working on a very simple piece, one that I did pretty well. But this time the choreographer was watching from behind us, so she could see the way my paralyzed heel kept rising off the mat. She kept yelling, "Heel down, Aaron!" I couldn't do it—it was simply not possible. She furiously signaled the accompanist to cut the music and stormed over to me and demanded to know why I wasn't listening to her, why she shouldn't just fire me on the spot for wasting everyone's time. The rehearsal hall was dead silent, full of other actors and technicians carefully trying not to overhear—which was, of course, impossible.

All I could do was reach down and pull up my pants leg so she could see the brace. Quietly, through clenched teeth I quietly said, "I can't." I wasn't fired, and she later wrote that "Aaron is phenomenal. One would never guess that a disabled person could do so much." The praise was like so many lead balls in my stomach.

I have always felt badly about that experience, and I especially regret how ashamed the choreographer obviously felt. She had no idea what was going on with me because I was deceiving her, deceiving everyone. But in that moment, my shame became her shame.

Another option for people with disabilities is to simply become invisible, and many of us try to do just that, aided by a society that encourages invisibility. Many of us experience terrible isolation, alienation, rejection and discrimination.

This church has been discussing putting in an elevator for some time now, and I am delighted to hear it. The accessibilities committee has been working hard to make the building more accessible for people with disabilities, and even though I am new here, it is clear that this is a community dedicated to being welcoming and inclusive. But the fact that you are even having this discussion now is because of the questionable moral actions of churches in the past.

The only reason every church in America is not fully accessible right now is because church groups successfully "lobbied for and received a blanket exemption from the Americans with Disabilities Act," effectively slamming church doors in the faces of millions of Americans. (Holmes A8) Many religious bodies have continued to think of and act as if access for persons with disabilities is a matter of benevolence and goodwill, rather than a prerequisite for equality and the foundation on which the church as model of justice must rest." (Eisland 67)

So bless you, First Unitarian Denver, for all that you have done and all you continue to do.

When I was in the wheelchair, I would often drive by buildings I was thinking about visiting. Stores, offices, even churches. I would carefully scan the building from the car. If it didn't look accessible or welcoming I would simply drive on. Nobody ever would have known I was there.

You see when I was looking at a building from the car—how accessible a building looked gave me information about how truly welcoming it was likely to be on the inside. I can't help but wonder how many people drive by churches all over America every Sunday.

I would have given anything to find a place where I was loved just as I was, a place where people saw the light of creation in my eyes. I would have wept to have found a community that would have stood with me and told all those people and groups and systems that tried to deny my full humanity to "leave our brother alone!"

I want every Unitarian Universalist congregation in the country to be such a place. I want our churches to stand as beacons of welcome for all people. I want our steeples to rise above the cities of America flying flags of inclusion and liberation. When people see our flaming chalices I want them to know that our flame is also their flame—without barrier or condition. This is my vision of full accessibility.

To embrace a vision of full accessibility is to embrace the imago dei, the face of God, in every person. It is to see our community enriched by the presence of people whose experiences and insights are far different, but no less valuable than our own. To embrace a vision of full accessibility is to live out our most sacred religious values, and to be an open door in a society full of closed doors. To embrace a vision of full accessibility is to radically widen and deepen our spiritual family, to find brothers and sisters where before we had only seen strangers.

May it be so. Amen. Blessed Be.

Facing Evil

Anne Barker
Student

Final Sermon in Evil, Trauma & Ambiguity class

What do we, as a liberal faith tradition, have to say about evil? What is it? How do we understand it? Is there anything we know for sure?

As a child, I was raised up in a Christian tradition where evil did not exist. God created the world, and it was good. Evil had no place in God's creation. What seemed to be evil was actually mortal error, misperception, thinking that needed to be corrected, waiting to be realigned with God's truth. The universe is created in the image and likeness of God, and is therefore perfect.

It was a nice way to grow up. I felt safe and confident that my needs would ultimately be met, that no obstacle was insurmountable, that the world was a friendly and negotiable place. From this, I retain some important beliefs about life: that I have the power to influence my own experience; that all life, actually all of existence, is sacred; that it is my responsibility to correct what is misaligned.

What I have left behind is the deep division between mind and body, the idea that the spiritual is real while the physical is unreal. It seems unreasonable to deny the evidence of the senses, to spend this life trying to overcome it. What I was left without was a theology of evil. After years of believing that it was my job to correct it, not to deny but to understand the nonexistence of it, now I had no way even to approach the subject. The world is good; what happens to that when I mix in evil?

There was also another problem in my way—the problem of compassion. The Bible tells us to love our neighbor, to turn the other cheek, to offer a hand of friendship and love. While I no longer consider myself a Christian, I am still deeply influenced by these roots. How can I name something evil, and remain consistent to the loving approach that I value so much?

I recommend that whenever you need to wrap your head around a deep theological problem, you go to lunch with your most thoughtful atheist friend. My atheist friend is the most theologically sound lay person I know. She even has some of the religious professionals beat.

My friend's approach is to consider evil from the idea of intent— that which is evil is done for malicious purposes, it is mean or violent or, in the very least, selfish. It is action taken with blatant disregard for the other. It is action designed to further the desires of the actor, with no care for anyone else who might be affected. This means that natural tragedies—hurricanes and earthquakes and the like—are not evil. They are terrible and devastating, but missing intent, they are not evil.

Still, I fought with her. Her stance sounded good, but couldn't it be said that there is some good in everyone? That something good arises out of every act? My very favorite fridge magnet says "Barn burnt down, now I can see the moon." It might be a tragedy that the barn is gone, but do we want to call it evil? Aren't we supposed to look for the moon?

After what seemed like hours, she finally figured out what was hanging me up. I was still too busy arguing to see it. "What is it that you are worried about losing?" she asked me.

That was it.

I was afraid that to name something evil, I was going to lose something far too precious to concede: I was going to lose my faith.

I have faith in the goodness of humans, the goodness in life itself, and that that we lean toward goodness. I cannot prove it in a double-blind, repeatable science experiment, but I believe it with my heart and mind. I have faith that while life is a glorious, messy, beautiful, terrible thing, we humans ultimately tend toward love.

I cannot speak to where we come from, or to where we go when that final breath leaves us, but I have experience with people and I have faith. Faith is not something that comes from somewhere, it is a choice we make. We place our faith on the notion most worthy to us and then we reinforce it with all the evidence that we can find.

Talking with my friend—trying to wrap my head around evil—I was afraid to lose that most tender kernel of faith that lives deepest within my heart. I believe in the inherent worth and dignity of every person—of every being. If I were to call one of those beings evil, what would happen to my belief? How can I believe in the inherent worth and dignity of evil?

This is best illustrated by the conversation we sometimes have about Hitler. Well, what about Hitler's inherent worth and dignity? What about that? Are we supposed to treat him the same as his millions of victims? Certainly Hitler is evil. The fact that we can even ask those questions tells me two things: that our Unitarian Universalist first principle is not a 'fact,' but is instead a statement of faith; and, that we are not all going to agree. What about Hitler? Is he evil?

In my lunch conversation, I began to understand my problem with evil. My friend pointed out that I see almost everything else on a spectrum or on a graduated scale, but I was seeing evil only as a strict polarity with good. If I was to call something evil, it could not be good. I do not do this with anything else, why was I doing it with evil? Why did I feel so threatened?

The other thing I discovered is that evil, as a noun, is inconsistent with my faith, my understanding of the world. I can not, will not, categorize a person as evil. I understand evil, instead, as a verb. It is not a being, but a doing. Hitler is responsible for horrific evil-doing, but I cannot call him evil. It is inconsistent with my faith.

I cannot call you evil, because to call you evil is to forget that we are both members of this tiny interdependent universe, beings seeking a meaningful life, love, happiness, safety. I cannot call you evil, because to do so is to draw a line, to put you on the other side, to cast you out of the community of faith and of hope. I cannot call you evil, because to-morrow it might be me, turning away from someone in need, ignoring gross injustice, wielding the death blow. I cannot call you evil, because to do so is to forget that you are a person, challenged by the limits to your knowledge, the limits to your understanding, the limits to your ability and the limits to your imagination. I cannot call you evil, because to do so would be to let you off the hook. I cannot call you evil, because to do so would be to let me off the hook. I cannot call you evil, because to do so would be to call all of humanity evil, because deep in the heart of my very being, I know that you and I are one.

Think, for a moment, about how you understand evil. Is it on a spectrum, or is it a polarity? What is on the other end? Is it goodness? Is it love? If evil is an action taken with negative intent, is the other side an action taken with positive intent? Perhaps that is more than good. Perhaps that positive intent means the other end is hope, or justice.

Maybe you do not see evil this way at all. Some people see it as a force in the world, a competing energy, attempting to triumph over love. Others see it as a noun, something, or someone, spoiled or broken. Do you have a philosophy, a theology, a psychological understanding of evil? Have you considered this?

There are as many stories in the world that illustrate depravity as there are stories that illustrate love. In a life with so many options, what will we choose? We can understand people many different ways, but it is what we lift up, what we shine light on, what we choose to believe, that tips the balance. There are thousands of years filled with stories of war, hunger, oppression and hate. There are thousands of years filled with stories of peace, generosity, triumph and love.

The Other Side of War by Zainab Salbi is filled with examples of human failing, of the ways we brutalize and torture and decimate the bodies and spirits of our earthly companions. It is also filled with tender stories of the rise of the human spirit, like a phoenix from the ashes, to rebuild and reclaim a sense of self in the face of seemingly insurmountable odds. What story will we lift up? Whose names will we remember? How will we make a difference?

We have taken the faith stance of recognizing the inherent worth and dignity of every person, and of asserting that every person should enjoy liberty and justice. Our liberal faith is inclusive and loving and generous and bold, but what does it have to help us in our encounters with evil? We enjoy the luxury of being theologians in one of the safest and most satisfying places on earth. It is easy to be an optimist or a pacifist in Canada. To be a Unitarian Universalist comes with negligible risk, to be queer does not incur state-sanctioned hanging, young people are not stolen into the army, or into the rebel forces, or into slavery. Not often. And yet, we will, each of us, encounter our share of evil. And how we respond will come out of how we have defined evil. This we know.

Coretta Scott King attended Unitarian churches for years. She and her husband, the Rev. Dr. Martin Luther King Jr., attended Unitarian churches together when they were in Boston. While he was in seminary, they considered this denomination for his future ministry. Mrs. King said:

> *We gave a lot of thought to becoming Unitarian at one*
> *time, but Martin and I realized we could never build a*
> *mass movement of black people if we were Unitarian.*
> *(McNatt)*

The Kings believed that they could not do what they needed to do, within this faith tradition. One of King's chief criticisms of liberal religion was that its theology of evil was too thin:

> *There is one phase of liberalism that I hope to cherish*
> *always: its devotion to the search for truth, its refusal to*
> *abandon the best light of reason. . . . It was . . . the*
> *liberal doctrine of man that I began to question. The*
> *more I observed the tragedies of history, and man's*
> *shameful inclination to choose the low road, the more I*

> *came to see the depths and strength of sin. ... I came
> to feel that liberalism had been all too sentimental
> concerning human nature and that it leaned toward a
> false idealism. I also came to see that liberalism's
> superficial optimism concerning human nature caused it
> to overlook the fact that reason is darkened by sin. ...
> Liberalism failed to see that reason by itself is little
> more than an instrument to justify man's defensive ways
> of thinking. Reason, devoid of purifying power of faith,
> can never free itself from distortions and rationaliza-
> tions. (McNatt)*

While we lift up the independent search for truth and meaning, what do we have to console victims of trauma, to comfort people who had been oppressed for generations and saw no end in sight, to inspire someone to challenge seemingly insurmountable odds? What do we have to meet the challenges of evil? Will believing in the goodness of people, and the right to freedom and justice, be enough? If we have no theology of evil, no way to understand the terrible bad things that people do to one another, how will we respond?

King had been known to quote Unitarian minister Theodore Parker, who first said, "I do not pretend to understand the moral universe; the arc is a long one... And from what I see I am sure it bends toward justice." (Manker-Seale) We are called, as people of faith, as citizens of the world, to see that arc—to celebrate the lean toward justice while witnessing the tragedies across the spectrum. We cannot afford the luxury of cherry-picking the happy stories and ignoring the suffering. To create an understanding of evil, to look at it and to approach it and to figure out how to ultimately wrestle with it, this is work we are called to do together. To turn away is to be victimized, to be blindsided. To hide is to live in fear. To work together, to take risks, to act, is to live out our faith with integrity.

Evil, in my understanding, is to damage or obscure a person's sense of self in such a way that they find themselves devoid of hope and love.

The response, then, is many layered. We must find ways to reach toward, to lift up, and to help those who are damaged or threatened. We must find ways to reach toward, to lift up, and to help those who are doing the damage or the threatening. We must find ways to change the structures of power in the world and in our communities, which encourage, provoke, and force people into states where evil-doing is an option.

To be effective in the world, to offer more than sunny optimism and a liberal religious cheering squad, we need to engage in the full spectrum of human existence. Each of us has a part to play: facing what frightens and perplexes us, finding our stance, wrestling with evil. To avoid it, to look away, even if we are looking reverently heavenward, is to invite evil in to fill the space left vacant. Choosing to not do the work is choosing to let evil-doing have the run of the universal farm. Allowing ourselves to be overwhelmed, rather than taking one small bite at a time, is to yield the world. When it comes to evil, there are no clean hands. We must, at the very least, look at what we hold in our own.

Theodore Parker also insisted that individuals "never violate the sacredness of your individual self-respect." King said, "Injustice anywhere is a threat to justice everywhere." Together, this forms the groundwork for the work we must do. To understand evil, as a community, we must hold strong to our individual self-respect, while remembering our place within the justice of the world. Let us overcome the optical delusion of our consciousness, free ourselves from our prisons, and widen our circle of compassion to embrace not only the rest of life and nature, but to clearly, intentionally include ourselves.

Flowers and Other Impractical Arrangements

Jessica Purple Rodela
Student

Horizon UU Church

July 9, 2006

While serving as a student chaplain last summer, I visited weekly with a bed-ridden woman who was—is still—dying by inches. I asked, as I always ask, what sustains her gracious spirit throughout the difficult days. She said she spent much of her time gazing at a stand of enormously tall sunflowers arranged precariously in an impractical vase on her windowsill. "Aren't they beautiful?" she asks. She tells me it gives her great comfort.

The visits reminded me of The Peace of Wild Things, a poem by Wendell Berry that I read as a prayer in my time of need. He writes:

> *When despair for the world grows in me*
> *and I wake in the night at the least sound*
> *in fear of what my life and my children's lives may be,*
> *I go and lie down where the wood drake*
> *rests in his beauty on the water, and the great heron*
>   *feeds.*
> *I come into the peace of wild things*

who do not tax their lives with forethought
of grief. I come into the presence of still water.
And I feel above me the day-blind stars
waiting with their light. For a time
I rest in the grace of the world, and am free.

The poet is right; nature sustains us, not just literally in the food we eat and the air we breathe. Nature sustains us spiritually as well. That sense of the "peace of wild things" occurs because in observing nature we are reminded that we humans are just one part of the vast construction and creation of the Universe. Observing nature reminds us that we are not separate, but interwoven into the very heart of this earth's machinations.

I felt the peace of wild things on a night gazing at stars near the Grand Canyon. I felt the peace of wild things in the call of gulls and the beating of the waves on the Texas coast. I felt the peace of wild things on a night at an anonymous lake, listening to the eerie song of loons. I felt the peace of wild things in the howling of coyotes in the California desert. I felt the peace of wild things gazing at a vase of sunflowers gathered by a woman's deathbed. What a paradox that for all the control we humans exert in our daily lives, we find comfort in the wilds of nature.

One morning in January, in the middle of a Chicago winter, I followed my dog down the steep steps of my apartment building into the backyard. I sat huddled in my coat, bored, waiting while my dog scampered through a foot of snow, sniffing attentively at each of a million unseen things. A squawking caught my attention, and I looked up to see two dozen, bright-green parrots huddled on the electrical lines strung above the alley. Puffed up against the cold, they look bigger than usual, an odd green against a blue and white sky, far from the familiar Argentinean sky that is their rightful home. Some few escaped or loosed birds have grown into a flock of 200 birds living in 15 sites in the South side of Chicago. Their nests are huge contraptions of paper and large twigs, they house multiple families of birds, keep them safe from the strong winds off Lake Michigan, and the months of freezing temperatures. A most impractical arrangement.

❋❋❋

The woman I visit gazes at sunflowers all day. Her illness has robbed her memory of continuity. She is dying by inches, and yet she attends to every inch, knowing each one matters, milking its mystery and savoring the salvation of every second. She looks away from me for awhile, and is startled to find me, a constant stranger, at her side. I introduce myself, again for me, the first time again for her, then tell her how much I admire the many paintings adorning the walls, the ones she has painted. She laughs when I call her an artist and directs my gaze to the REAL art in the room—those magnificent sunflowers arranged by the picture window. She smiles and says, "Aren't they beautiful?" It's not a question so much as a reminder to pay attention.

❋❋❋

Attention deficit disorder is no new phenomenon. In the ancient wisdom of the Bhagavad-Gita, the Warrior Arjuna laments to his god: "Krishna, the mind is faltering, violent, strong, and stubborn; I find it as difficult to hold as the wind." I had lived in Chicago for a full year before I paid attention to the parrots in Nichols Park. Every morning and every evening, my walk to and from my work at the lakeshore retirement home took me through the middle of that park, and on a particularly difficult day, a day spent facing despair and fearing death, I looked up to see not the expected city pigeons, but bright green parrots. Those parrots, strung across the park like so many gems, are there for just the price of my attention.

I walked through that park every day over the summer, and decided that everyday I would pay the price of attention as a toll on every walk through Nichols Park. And so I walked every day, to work, on the way to visit a woman who is dying by inches.

❋❋❋

The woman I visit, this patient patient, whose illness has robbed her of the memory of movement, gazes at sunflowers all day. I return every week, to a ritual of re-introduction. And I recite a litany of our connections: the Unitarian minister she remembers; the senior chaplain she trusts; the grown daughters she relies on. Then she introduces me to the sunflowers, huge, improbable vase-clad stalks in the window. Aren't they beautiful, she asks, and makes a believer out me. I pay attention, again for the first time, and I am born again.

***

It took 16 years for Mark Bittner to pay attention. The book and documentary film called "The Wild Parrots of Telegraph Hill" tells the story of self-styled 'dharma bum' Mark Bittner, who spent six years befriending a flock of some 25 wild parrots nesting in San Francisco. Mark had pined away in the city, had spent years planning how to relocate to the country, into the "wild." At a point of feeling spiritually bereft and helplessly displaced, Mark read the work of Gary Snyder, a poet and environmentalist. Snyder wrote: "The city is just as natural as the country, let's not forget it. There's nothing in the universe that's not natural by definition."

Mark's self-pity so challenged, he set about to discover the wildlife of the city, particularly its birds, and then particularly its parrots; and in paying daily attention to the flock of displaced cherry-headed conures, Mark came to understand, respect, then love them; ultimately he learned to distinguish the parrots as individuals. In return, for the mere price of paying attention to parrots, Mark learned what it was he loved, and learned to love his life again. Perhaps that's the goal we seek when we say we want more spirituality: learning to love our own lives again.

Years before, Mark Bittner had identified three keys to his contentment: love, vocation, and location. He was surprised to find that once he paid attention to this moment, to his "now," that the answer was right there, surrounding him.

One day, Mark looked up from his bird feeding perch to see his literary hero, Gary Snyder, headed right toward him. Gary Snyder! The man whose challenge to find the natural in the city as well as the country had captured Mark's attention; the man whose challenge had led to finding 'the peace of wild things' there in his own backyard; the challenge which had led to writing as the work he loved about the things he came to love; the writing which had led to his falling in love with the film-maker who brought his own story to national attention. *That* Gary Snyder was walking toward him and soon standing right before him, asking to see the parrots. Mark reeled off his usual introductions and explanations given to tourists hundreds of times, and then finally admitted, "I know who you are. ... It's amazing to see you here. ... Before I read you, I never knew what any of the birds or the trees or the flowers were called. Now I'm learning their names."

The poet smiled and nodded at Mark. "It's only polite," he said.

✸✸✸

The woman I visit pays attention to sunflowers all day. She would not remember me now, did not remember me then. I explain that I am a colleague sent by her Unitarian minister. Her eyes light up in recognition: "You know the Reverend? Are you a Unitarian Universalist, too?"

It is a coincidence, to her, worth paying attention to, every time we meet for the first time again. She has faith in our connections. I once asked her if she believed in God. "Oh," she said, "of course I believe in flowers." She directs my gaze to the stand of sunflowers in the window. I don't know how they get there, the sunflowers; I don't know who replenishes them or where they come from. But I have faith, faith that every week sunflowers will adorn the windowsill.

"Aren't they beautiful?" she asks.

I tell her: "They feel like a prayer to me, always facing the light, in hopeful expectation of sunlight just beyond their grasp and gaze."

✸✸✸

This summer I stand daily in the yard, and look up, shielding my eyes from the sharp summer sun. There are herons there, nesting high in the trees in my suburban yard in Coppell. One morning I saw the young birds, mouths yawing, clearly yapping for food, but I could not hear their cries. And that's when I noticed the sound, a background din that had been near-constant during my vigil with the birds, a whirring blur of a noise that crescendos and falls like a buzzing sprinkler head watering dry grass. I remember the sound from childhood visits home to grandmother's house: the sound of Texas' dog-day cicadas, come out for the summer cycle.

Cicadas live a double life. They spend years, from two to 17, as subterranean grubs before hatching into a winged buggy prehistoric flying form. I've not seen one yet, but I hear their persistent song following the ebb and flow of the day's weather.

I pay attention; I pray; and it is as though these things come into being. They were always there, of course, but they were not there for me until I noticed.

The Huron Indians have a word for such a prayer: orenda. At its root, orenda means merely "song," but particularly the whirring crackling song of the cicadas. Orenda.

The Hurons believed the cicadas' morning song to be an incantation to ensure that the sun will shine brightly on the earth and allow the corn to ripen properly. As such, the word became a synonym for "prayer."

Orenda is not quite so passive as the conventional meaning of "prayer," because it also carries a charge that we are in some way, through the interconnectedness of all things, able to exert some influence—not manipulation—but influence. So, you would say that I am "arrayed in my own orenda;" that is, I hope or expect. It conveys intention, not passivity; it recognizes that what we pay attention to matters; our way of thinking about our lives influences how we feel and how we cope with the circumstances of our lives. Orenda acknowledges that though we are not in control, neither are we powerless. Prayer in this sense, as orenda, proffers no refuge, but a way to take charge and sort through our priorities, focusing our attention on what is important to us, whether expressed through hopes, fears, gratitude, or desire.

Orenda reconciles the apparent paradox of prayerful atheists such as myself. I'm often asked, if I am an atheist, who it is I pray to. But they misunderstand my intent. I do not pray to anyone, I pray to connect. And connection is as simple as paying attention. I pay attention, thus I learn to love.

Arranging flowers in a vase: that's a prayer. Cooking a meal for my family is a prayer. Smiling at a stranger is a prayer. Sitting with my coffee in the backyard I look up at—oh, can you believe it? Herons, nesting in the banality of suburbia. Now, that's a prayer.

*****

We are surrounded by the impossible. When we notice it, we deem it a miracle. But when we pay attention, we experience grace—a saving grace, an amazing grace, a grace abounding, a grace that sustains us.

*****

Reverend William Schulz writes:

> *"It is not a distant, mysterious God to whom we make appeal or even the cold vagaries of Progress, Evolution, Creativity, or History. The gods and goddesses—or, if you prefer, the most precious and profound—are accessible to us in the taste of honey and the touch of stone. And this in turn is why we love the earth, honor the human body, and bless the stars. Religion is not just a matter of Things Unseen. For us the Holy's not hidden but shows its face in the blush of the world's exuberance." (Lach 37)*

*****

The woman I visit faces a window, gazing at sunflowers. Though we have been introduced, again for the first time, she tells me her name. She offers me hospitality from her deathbed with a flourish of refined manners. She introduces herself to me, then to the sunflowers on the windowsill.

"Aren't they beautiful?" she asks.

I reply: "They look . . . impossible."

Or do I mean improbable? Most of the sunflower is seeds, no flower at all. She and I talk about the improbability of sunflowers. She asks—again for me, the first time for her—of the certitude of her coming death. I reassure her with flowers. I tell her that for Unitarian Universalists nature is a reminder that we are all part of a great interdependent web of being. We humans, each one of us, every star, each drop of water, every sunflower, we are all made of the same stuff.

The dying woman smiled at me and said, "Why, then, we are all seeds, aren't we? Planted and growing in one beautiful garden."

May it be so.

And the Wall
Came Tumbling Down

India McCanse
Student

Unitarian Church North Mequon, Wisconsin

August, 2006

I'd like to invite you to take a tour with me into a series of rooms which illustrate the breadth of our topic.

Room I

We join a meeting going on in an enormous hall where powerful men are debating serious issues. The summer light shines through the high windows and pipe and cigar smoke is thick. Some of these men are concerned about individual beliefs and conscience and others believe all the answers are found in the one true religion with a God that permeates the very essence of all existence. They are from varied faiths and traditions and represent numerous political, geographic and religious interests. They are debating a previously enacted document that some now think should be changed. One man, seemingly in a leadership position, steps to the podium and is politely recognized.

"Gentlemen," he begins. "I submit that in the process of creating our national governance, we have escaped our duty to protect the individual liberties of those we represent." Mr. Madison continued, "And so, with this burdensome weight from having done so, I present to you ten new clauses for insertion to our constitution, which I have labeled, the Bill of Rights." The hall was filled with echoing noise—angry shouts as well as praise for this man's courage. Madison yells over the chaos, "The amendments which have occurred to me, proper to be recommended by Congress to the State Legislatures are these...That in article 1st, section 9, insert "The civil rights of none shall be abridged on account of religious belief or worship, nor shall any national religion be established ..."

Room 2

In a small, warm hospital room, she lays calmly in bed. Her eyes are open. He reflects on their life together but mostly on the last few weeks. He remembers the great times, vacations, biking, skipping dinner and going upstairs. Only a nurse and his brother are with him but hundreds are gathered outside. It seems unreal that so many are involved. That this crowd of people who don't even know them become intimately involved in their family crisis. Months ago, a State judge ruled that Michael had the right, as Terri's husband, to remove her feeding tube. Since then, numerous appellate and federal court decisions delayed an intervention. The state legislature passed "Terri's Law" and the U.S. Supreme Court refused six times to hear the case. The President of the United States signed a bill that would let federal judges hear the case, but none would. From this warm hospital room, Michael Schiavo watched the President on CNN. Mr. Bush remarked, "The essence of civilization is that the strong have a duty to protect the weak. In cases where there are serious doubts or questions, the presumption should be in favor of life." (CNN.com)

It was hard to tell where the church stopped and the state began in this whole scenario; they were hopelessly intermingled. "She's gone Mr. Schiavo," the nurse said as she exited Terri's room.

Room 3

At Chris and Mary's house, their daughter Kayla loves to play in the back yard. She has a large swing, a sandbox and a Playskool playground. She often has friends over and Chris is vigilant at making sure Kayla plays safely. Both Mary and Chris are employed so Kayla goes to day care. In this house, everyone is careful because they can't afford health insurance. They don't qualify for any assistance so they must do their best to avoid accidents. Mary makes slightly more than Chris but taxes in this state are high so the amount left for the household is minimal after the $150 a week for child care. Chris is employed by a conservative Christian school and is a fine teacher, but they don't treat Chris very well. God forbid something should happen to Mary. If she died, her partner Chris would have no legal right to Kayla, though she's been "Mom" since Kayla was born. Chris cannot tell her employer she is lesbian or they will remove her. The school teaches that homosexuality is a sin and threatens the institutions of family and marriage.

Room 4

In a warm, candlelit, simple kitchen, the family gathers around the table for the evening meal. Prayers are offered. The son addresses his dad, 'But it's against the law father, the police will come and arrest you."

"There is no law higher than God's Law," the father responds.

"Yes, father" the son replies. His mother, standing behind him with the other women, puts more food on the table. The final letter had come from the state and was glowing in the candlelight on the table.

"Then let them arrest me," the father spoke. This Amish family did become a test case before the high Court because, to the Yoders, it was contrary to their religious beliefs for their children to attend public high school. They argued that attending eight grades of formative public teaching would give their children the basis they needed for education. Beyond that was, in their view, the government forcing their children to be exposed to a world outside of which they chose to live.

Room 5

The last room is a room I was in about five months ago. My agency, Big Brothers Big Sisters, was awarded a large federal grant for mentoring children of incarcerated parents. I have a powerful and well connected Board member that called me one day and said, "Cancel your calendar for next Thursday, I'm taking you to the White House."

Now, what does one say to one's employer when one feels so very strongly in opposition to those who live there? I thanked him and got off the phone. My Board Member had invited me to attend the White House Conference on the Office of Faith Based Initiatives. This Office was created by an Executive Order of the President after a Congressional bill failed to muster enough support to be passed. This Office was run by Director, James Touhy, an ardent Catholic attorney who had only one client his whole life: a woman called Mother Theresa.

The purpose of my visit was to attend the conference, where the President was the keynote, and then speak with White House staffers about our program (which was second largest in the country). I actually took it as my duty to ensure that this program would be re-funded, as we were coming to the third year of funding.

On the second day, in an office in the White House complex, I was welcomed by staff in Mr. Touhy's office. "He's with Mr. Rove right now, won't you have a seat."

Just keep breathing was all I could think. As I glanced around the room there were poster-sized photos everywhere: one of the cabinet together in prayer; and one of Mr. Bush, Mr. Cheney, Mr. Rumsfeld and Dr. Rice in a morning Bible study.

Finally, I was invited upstairs to Mr. Touhy's office. He was predictably on the phone. I stopped in my tracks. Above him was an enormous photograph that haunts me still. It was a larger than life picture of the top of a head and some hands folded together. The hair was grey, the eyes were closed and the fingers were interlaced. I suddenly realized I was staring at a picture of the President of the United States kneeling in prayer on the wall of the White House. I couldn't take my eyes off of it.

I had long since stopped breathing. I pulled my jaw all the way off the floor as Mr. Touhy got off the phone. He asked some questions and then handed me over to a special assistant to the President who asked me more questions. It was clear there was little to no understanding about the plight of these hidden children.

I was there three and a half hours. I left the reception area staring back at the photos once more and stepped out into a sunny spring DC morning. How is it possible that so much religion, so much Christianity, could be so present in such a sacredly secular space?

I want to make clear that I am not criticizing an individual or a political party. Other elected officials from other parties have drawn religion into state affairs before. I do take exception to the concept of establishing, supporting or funding religion in government affairs. I submit we have never seen it to the degree we do now. Let me provide a few more examples.

Author Michelle Goldberg, in her book, Kingdom Coming: the Rise of Christian Nationalism, provides historic and compelling insights about the shrinking of the wall. My experience of the White House is beautifully laid out in her chapter called the "Faith Based Gravy Train."

The diversion of billions of dollars from secular social service agencies to religious outfits has been one of the most underreported stories of this administration, Goldberg asserts. The Office of Faith Based Initiatives has become a major source of funding for evangelical ministries, which are now involved in everything from prison programs and job training to teenage pregnancy prevention, supplanting the safety net that was supposed to catch all Americans. As a result of these initiatives, it has been documented that a growing number of social service jobs have refused to hire Jews, gays and other undesirables. Bringing the dispossessed to Christ has become something very close to a domestic policy goal for this administration.

In March of last year, the President proudly told a conference of religious leaders that the federal government gave two billion dollars in grants to faith based groups the year before. In 2003, the total was

$1.7 billion and this year, the number is on the rise. Recently, I received an email from the Department of Health and Human Services announcing the awarding of $118 million in grants to promote 'Healthy Marriage' (that would be *heterosexual* marriage) and Fatherhood Initiatives. The summary reported that 225 grantees had received funding (an average of $525,000 each) to help couples form and sustain healthy marriages and equip men to be involved, responsible and committed fathers. It further stated that this set of grants came from the Temporary Assistance for Needy Families (TANF) Act that used to provide funding for emergency shelter, housing, food and indigent health care.

Don't get me wrong, I'm all for healthy marriages, and who better to direct a healthy marriage program than our federal government? And yes, it seems now we have a way to make fathers more committed, more responsible and more available to their children. Alternatively I suppose, we could take those TANF dollars and spend on job training to help those fathers provide for their children.

The Associated Press conducted a study of 1600 grantees of faith based organizations since the office was established and found that only 50 were Jewish, five were Muslim, and one was Buddhist. Examples of grantees include Pat Robertson's Operation Blessing, receiving $1.5 million; funding for the nation's first "faith-based prison" in Florida (as requested by the President's brother); and $400,000 for three years to Atlanta's Youth for Christ, to hire abstinence educators. There are no requirements for degrees or credentials, but employees do have to be Christian. Their website says "The mission of Youth for Christ is to participate in the body of Christ in responsible evangelism of youth … then discipling them into the local church." This federal grant doubled their budget.

In 1997, then Governor Bush pushed through legislation exempting faith-based facilities from regulations applying to their secular counterparts. State licensing and credentialing for religious drug treatment counselors, child care workers and other religious social service employees would be waived under this measure. It backfired. Four years after

Governor Bush freed Christian residential child care facilities from state supervision, the mother of an 18-year-old boy who had rescued her son from a south Texas Boys Home, was told by an emergency room doctor, "Ma'am, your son has been tortured." The headmaster was found guilty of abuse. Later, his wife was legally banned from ever working with children again because of her treatment of a girl at a faith-based facility. The girl was bound with duct tape, kicked in the ribs and locked in a closet for 32 straight hours while loud recordings of the headmaster's sermons played continuously.

These are extreme examples. And there is no question that thousands of faith-based entities do great works in our country. Our own UU congregations are great examples of this. But religious beliefs cannot and should not be the credentials one needs for employment. Nor should public funds (our tax dollars) ever be used to prostheletise or establish a religious point of view. That's what the wall was for.

Unitarian Universalism is a religious tradition that espouses freedom, reason and tolerance. In my view, that is:

- the freedom to believe and practice whatever faith or spiritual tradition one wishes, without discrimination or harm being brought because of those beliefs;
- the reason to invite our minds to engage in self conversation about what makes sense religiously; and,
- the tolerance to accept, embrace and comprehend the rich and diverse beliefs and traditions of others.

Our forefathers labored to craft a document that would protect those freedoms from anyone, any state or any power that might remove them. This is the essence of Unitarian Universalism, our ability to reason for ourselves, to embrace the beliefs of others, rather than having them believe as we do. I think that's what Thomas Jefferson meant when, in his famous letter to the Danbury Baptists, he said, "Believing with you that religion is a matter which lies solely between man and his God …

I contemplate with sovereign reverence that act of the whole American people which declared that their legislature should 'make no law respecting an establishment of religion or prohibiting the free exercise thereof,' thus building a wall of separation between Church and State." (Wilson 74) It was Jefferson who coined the phrase "a wall of separation."

I suggest that when a government takes on the responsibility of interpreting scripture (or any sacred text) or claims to know the answers to the largest or most personal questions, that government becomes a theocracy, and by definition removes the wall between church and state, while massively overstepping its authority. It is a government that is not "of the people or by the people," it is a government driven by one group's interpretation of beliefs and principles, not those agreed to in the bill of rights.

When any religious beliefs are forced on others, there is born a state of tyranny. But it goes far beyond just beliefs. The actions behind those beliefs can lead to the torture of a young man in a boy's home; to a girl being bound and locked in a closet for religious "programming" and those actions can lead to the extinction of millions of humans or entire civilizations through war.

That's why the wall is imperative; that's why the wall must stand; and that's why our forefathers labored to get it right, in that smoke-filled room in the first place.

A Cancer on Our Democracy: What I Saw in Guantanamo

Justin Osterman, DMin '99

Unity Temple, Oak Park, Illinois

October 2006

In August of 2005 I spent five days at the United States Naval Base in Guantanamo Bay, Cuba. I went there to interpret for two attorneys representing prisoners who are being held in our nation's so-called "War on Terror." That trip earned me the distinction of being the first non-military clergy-person to meet and speak with prisoners in Guantanamo Bay. It may well be that I am the only civilian minister to have ever done so. That experience has given me a unique insight into the experience of the prisoners in that facility and my study both in preparation for the trip and subsequent to it—as well as my reflections on all that I have seen and learned—has led me to the conclusion that the greatest threat facing our American democracy at this point in our nation's history is posed not by foreign religious extremists who hate America, but rather by the fear-inspired policies and laws that have been adopted since September 11th, 2001, in the name of safe-guarding our nation.

The Guantanamo Bay prison is a blight on our nation's image in the world, a stain on our country's moral credibility, and a threat to the very democracy that the men and women of our nation's military are honor-bound to defend. I submit to you today that the Guantanamo prison is the visible manifestation of a secretive and cancerous growth within our democracy that is a threat to the principles of our political system, a threat to the foundations of our legal system, a threat to our national security, and a threat to the very moral fabric of our nation.

Before I go on, you should know this about me: I am a lifelong Unitarian Universalist and I am an Army veteran trained to read, write, and speak Arabic. I served in Military Intelligence and was an interpreter with a peacekeeping force in the Middle East. On September 11th, 2001, three members of the religious community I serve were in the north tower of the World Trade Center; two of them were father and son. Two men escaped the tower; 25-year-old Todd Joseph Ouida was not one of them. I conducted his memorial service before his grief-stricken father, one of the two survivors. I live with the memory of September 11th everyday of my life. I assure you that my desire to see those responsible for that attack and my determination to prevent another such tragedy on American soil are second to none. Because of that, I supported our nation's military action in Afghanistan, as did nearly the entire international community.

But what I have seen done in our nation, and in our names, since then has left me outraged and fearful for the future of this great American democratic experiment.

I hardly need recount the litany of reactivity here in America over the past five years: enactment of the USA Patriot Act; the creation of secret prisons around the world in which brutal, coercive interrogation techniques are sanctioned by our government; the kidnapping by our intelligence services of foreign nationals and their open-ended imprisonment without legal justification for their seizure or recourse to their detention; the creation of secret military tribunals, in which the accused sees neither his accusers nor the evidence against him, the verdicts of which are not reviewable by our judicial system; unlawful, secret domestic wire-tapping; and the declaration of US citizens as "enemy combatants," a hitherto unknown legal classification that our government has used to deny them the basic human, civil, and legal rights guaranteed to us by the Constitution of this nation.

Friends, I see a nation that has lost its moral bearing and is at risk of becoming a caricature of a functioning democracy and a shadowy vision of some the very regimes that our nation has historically—and at times heroically—opposed. I submit to you that policies that gave rise to and the current laws that make legitimate the prison in Guantanamo pose a far greater threat to our nation than any of the men currently being held in that facility in our names.

It has been proven beyond any doubt that the horrific abuses that occurred in the Abu Ghraib prison in Iraq were not the result of a "few bad apples" in our military, but, rather, were the logical result of the policies that led to and the tactics that were perfected in Guantanamo Bay, Cuba. We've all seen the pictures: naked men being treated like animals, hooded, terrorized by attack dogs, threatened with bodily harm. Every one of these same abuses was a part of established interrogation techniques in Guantanamo before they were exported to Iraq.

If there was no Guantanamo, there would have been no Abu Ghraib. The tortured legal interpretations that allowed Guantanamo to exist and evolve, undergirded the abuse in Iraq. Whatever you think about our nation's involvement in Iraq, I think we can all agree that the abuse in the Abu Ghraib prison shamed our nation, endangered our military personnel in Iraq, and undermined US national security interests. We owe this to the existence of Guantanamo.

To add insult to injury, some of the architects of the policies that led to Abu Ghraib still occupy positions of power and prestige in our government, while some of the junior enlisted women and men who implemented these policies occupy cells in federal prison. That is a moral travesty and, as a former Army non-commissioned officer, I am outraged by this staggering injustice.

While I was at the prison in Cuba, I spent nearly as much time around the guards as I did talking with the prisoners. As a former Army sergeant, I struck up an easy rapport with the guards and found them to be decent, honorable citizen soldiers. After a few days, the word got out that—in addition to being a veteran—I was a minister. One day a young guard approached and asked me, "Is it true that you're a pastor?" I replied, "Yes." The guard said, "I'd like to talk with you." Then, to my surprise, the guard turned around and walked away. Confused at first, I followed the guard around a corner to a spot in which no one could see or hear us talking. The guard turned to me and, in a low voice, said, "I know that there are some prisoners here who want to have attorneys, but don't know how to get in touch with one. They ask me if I can help them, and I don't know what to do. Pastor, what should I do?"

Friends, we have placed a generation of patriotic Americans—committed to defending our democracy—in situations that require them to violate the very morals and principles of democracy that they are pledged to defend. That is wrong.

What troubles me most deeply is how far we have strayed, driven by fear and in the name of national security, from the values and ideals for which our great nation stands. For generations, America has led the way in advancing the causes of international law, civil rights, and human rights; we have championed individual liberty, fundamental fairness, and impartial justice in civil societies. These values and ideals are our birthright and our heritage.

Over the past five years, our nation has retreated from every one of these basic American values. We have embarrassed ourselves as a society by allowing systematic abuses to take place in our names; we have driven from our side all but our most tenacious allies in the world; we have squandered all the sympathy and moral credibility the world conferred on us after September 11, 2001; we have antagonized neutral populations and created enemies where none previously existed, and we have violated the simple standards of decency for which our great nation stands. It is a travesty bordering on criminality. And there has been criminal behavior which has gone unchecked and unchallenged.

Our democratic system of checks and balances is neither checking the abuse of individuals and of power nor maintaining the balance of power between the branches of our government. The Military Commission Act, which was signed into law less than two weeks ago, bestows unprecedented power on the executive branch of the government and fundamentally limits the power of the judicial branch. Rather than insist that our government abide by its own laws, we accept illegality in the name of security and amend our laws to make criminal acts policy.

Supreme Court Justice Louis Brandeis wrote in 1928, "In a government of laws, existence of the government will be imperiled if it fails to observe the law scrupulously. ... If the government becomes the law-breaker, it breeds contempt for law. ... To declare that in the administration of the criminal law the end justifies the means—to declare that the government may commit crimes in order to secure the conviction of a private criminal—would bring terrible retribution." (dissenting opinion in Olmstead v. United States)

If, pacified by fear, we allow the government to violate our established standards of conduct and decency, then our very society is in peril. Founding father Benjamin Franklin's words haunt me these days: "Those who would sacrifice liberty for security deserve neither." Our government has twice declared its own citizens (Yasir Hamdi and Jose Padilla) "enemy combatants" and imprisoned them in violation of their constitutional rights. In 2002, the CIA killed another US citizen in Yemen (Ahmed Hijazi) with a Hellfire missile fired from a Predator drone.

Army Captain, and Muslim Chaplain, James Yee, whom I had the privilege of meeting in person last year, served at the prison in Cuba for nearly a year. A West Point graduate, he was arrested upon leaving Guantanamo, hooded, shackled, and publicly accused of (but never charged with) espionage, threatened with the death penalty, and held in solitary confinement for 76 days, without access to an attorney. When all was said and done, two minor disciplinary charges—having nothing to do with espionage—were leveled at Captain Yee, both of which were rescinded, and he was given a medal for his service in Guantanamo.

United States citizens have been and are being treated exactly the way we are treating the prisoners in Guantanamo: arrested, interrogated without an attorney, imprisoned without charges, and then quietly released when no evidence of a crime can be produced. And the dubious legality behind this imprisonment of U.S. citizens without charges is inextricably intertwined with the immorality that allows the prison in Guantanamo to exist. We have exported Guantanamo to Iraq and imported it into the United States.

And while the prisoners in Guantanamo are characterized as the "worst of the worst," all guilty by virtue of mere accusation, a summary of U.S. government reports on the status of prisoners in Guantanamo, compiled by Unitarian attorney Josh Denbeaux, revealed that more than half of the prisoners have not been determined to have committed any hostile act against our nation or its allies. Nearly nine out of every 10 were seized by Afghani or Pakistani forces after substantial bounties were offered for the capture of al-Qaida and Taliban members.

Most of the approximately 400 prisoners who are still being held in the Guantanamo prison are entering their fifth year of imprisonment, and only 10 have been charged with a crime. The harsh circumstances of their open-ended imprisonment are inhumane and a fundamental violation of everything that our nation stands for, legally and morally. The interrogation methods to which some of them have been subjected include physical assault, sexual humiliation, and purposeful religious insults. We now know that a team of military medical and scientific personnel, including psychiatrists and psychologists, has been working at Guantanamo to "assist the interrogators" (New Yorker, 11 & 18 July 2005) while denying prisoners basic medical and dental care. You may not call this torture, but I call it un-American.

In March 2006—and only by court order—our government finally began releasing the names of Guantanamo prisoners. I can tell you two names: Rafiq and Muhammad. These are the Tunisian men with whom I met. To the American public they are just objects in white, beige, or orange jumpsuits appearing on the evening news. But to me, they are husbands, brothers, sons, and cousins. They are human beings. And the treatment to which they have been subjected is inhumane. They are confined in cages no larger than a generous walk-in closet in a suburban

American home. When they leave their cells, they are shackled hand, foot, and waist. If they refuse to leave their cells for interrogation, they are "forcibly extracted" by a five-man team of guards wearing protective gear and bearing riot shields. If they protest their open-ended imprisonment by going on hunger strike, they are restrained in chairs and force fed by having feeding tubes forced down their noses and into their stomachs. Friends, the animals in the Brookfield Zoo are treated better than these men are and this is shameful.

Shameful.

When a hopeless, despairing prisoner in Guantanamo commits suicide, our government dismisses it as a propaganda ploy and as an act of "asymmetrical warfare."

Muhammad knows the feeling of hopelessness and despair. Years ago, he fled the repressive government in Tunisia to make a better life in Europe. Unable to find a place for himself in western society—a familiar story, if you've been watching the world news for the past year—he moved to Pakistan, where he started a honey business, and married. In the months following the U.S. attack on Afghanistan, he was riding in a truck, on his way to buy medication for his wife, when he was arrested by Pakistani forces and sold to the Americans in Afghanistan for $5,000. He has a weak heart, kidney problems, and suffers from a number of chronic diseases. By our government's own account, they have no reason to believe he ever was or is now a threat to anyone, but he is entering his fifth year in Guantanamo ... arrested for a bounty, imprisoned on suspicion, never charged with a crime, and subjected to ruthless interrogation. This is unconscionable ... and it is being done in our names.

But our government does not want you to know about Muhammad as a valuable, unique human being, with hopes, fears, and rights—a human being just like you and like me. He, and every other prisoner in Guantanamo Bay, has value to our government, not as a source of actionable intelligence as some would claim, but as a symbol and an object. A symbol of the undeclared and unending "War on Terror" that we are reminded of daily and as an object of fear. The minute he is seen and experienced by us as a three-dimensional human being, he will cease to be of any value to our government. In fact, if we experienced him as a subject, then his on-going incarceration would create a problem for our nation.

That is why the newly-enacted Military Commission Act includes a provision that would prevent prisoners like Muhammad from challenging the grounds of their imprisonment in Guantanamo. On the day the Act was signed, the Justice Department moved to have all the Habeas Corpus lawsuits, filed on behalf of prisoners, thrown out of federal court.

You all know the symbol of democracy in our country, right? It's a woman wearing a blindfold holding the scales of justice in one hand. In this land, justice is supposed to be blind, not us, the citizens, blind to injustice being perpetrated in our names.

Justice isn't blind in America today: she's hooded, shackled, and held in solitary confinement with the attack dogs of extremism and fear snarling in her face and snapping at her heels—and in the faces and at the heels of any decent, patriotic American who dares speak out for truth, fairness, and mercy in this land.

Seeing every human being as unique and inherently worthy is precisely what Jesus admonishes us to do in the Gospel of Matthew. Whether it be by a dispenser of cosmic justice or by the unflinching eye of history, every nation will be judged for its actions, "[b]efore him will be gathered all the nations, and he will separate them one from another as a shepherd separates the sheep from the goats."

And the measure of any society and its people will be its treatment of and regard for the most vulnerable of those in its charge, be they its sons or strangers, its daughters or its detainees. I think of Muhammad languishing in that prison, stripped of his human dignity, ailing and alone in a cell and the words of the Gospel whisper in my heart, "'Lord, when ... did we see thee naked and clothe thee? And when did we see thee sick or in prison and visit thee?" And the King will answer them, "... as you did it to one of the least of these my brethren, you did it to me.'"

Guantanamo Bay, Cuba, is our prison: it is your prison and it is my prison. All that has been done in that prison has been done in our names. And I, for one, cannot accept this any longer. Not in my name.

We face a moral turning point in our nation's history; we will either excise the disease that is spreading from Guantanamo and threatening our American way of life, or we will succumb as a society to its ravages and the American way of life as we know it will die. As patriotic citizens and people of faith, we must demand the immediate closure of the Guantanamo prison and insist that the sterilizing light of open and public examination be brought to bear not just on the prison itself, but on the policies and persons that have allowed this facility to exist.

The future of our nation, and all for which it stands, is at stake.

Beyond Iraq

Matt Tittle, MDiv '04

Bay Area Unitarian Universalist Church

August 16, 2006

Unless we demand change in a troubled world, change will not come. I stand here this morning with a heavy heart—less hopeful than I would like and more sorrowful than usual. But I also stand before you with great conviction that the time has come to say enough and to demand that the U.S. government change its current course of pre-emptive violence before it is too late. The great abolitionist Frederick Douglass said:

> *Power concedes nothing without a demand. It never did and never will. Find out what people will submit to, and you have found out the exact amount of injustice which will be imposed upon them. The limits of tyrants are prescribed by the endurance of those whom they op-press. (Douglass 579)*

I have never been so concerned that violence around the globe would escalate into an uncontrollable world conflict. Violence has esca-lated in the Middle East to a point where we stand realistically on the brink of world war as Israel fights on two fronts against both Hezbollah and Hamas; as Iran supplies not only Hezbollah, but cooperates with North Korea; as both Iran and North Korea respond with defiance to western demands to control their nuclear capabilities; as other nuclear powers like China and India demand their fair share of the world's resources of which the United States uses a disproportionate amount; as terrorism increases around the world; and as the United States finds itself bogged down in Iraq, which stands perilously close to a civil war.

I believe history will count the Iraq War as one of the greatest mistakes of the U.S. government. We must look beyond Iraq in shaping a world in which military force is used only as a last resort and only in self -defense or in defense of another. We must look beyond Iraq in shaping a world where terrorism is irrelevant because the conditions in which terrorism flourishes are absent. Preemptive warfare, like that launched in Iraq, without provocation and without just cause, will continue to result in increased violence and terror around the world because it fuels the causes of terrorism.

The nation and the world are on the verge of a new era—a new global reality that will define our future, that of our children, and their children. Over the past few centuries, we have shrunk our world into a global community in terms of information, commerce, international relations, and transportation. We are a global village, but we have not learned to live in global peace and justice. That is our task as people of faith, as Americans, and as inhabitants of this earth.

I come to my views on war in general and this war in particular based largely on my own twenty years of military service in the Navy, most of which were as an intelligence officer and include a graduate degree in national security affairs; brief combat action in Grenada and Lebanon; being privy to the details and execution of the 1991 Gulf War as an intelligence analyst in Washington, DC; working as a nuclear weapons inspector in Russia and as an arms control negotiator with the Russians and Ukrainians. I have spent most of my adult life as a student and facilitator of international relations with a clear understanding of the role of military action. My views are my own, but I trust that I have arrived at them with some practical expertise. I come to them also from the perspective of someone who has dedicated his life more recently to the vocation of caring for the soul and working to create the beloved community.

Based on my experience, I have been preaching against the Iraq War since before it began. Many Americans make a direct link between the events of September 11, 2001 and the war in Iraq because our government has made a concerted effort to speak often of them in the same breath. Although the two events are not directly related, this is a case where believing something all but makes it so. The events of September 11, 2001 sparked a fear of the other that led to a deafening silence among the people of this nation in 2003, when President Bush made his case for invading Iraq. This silence went beyond the people, although not all of us were silent. Many of us spoke out loudly, but we were condemned as unpatriotic when we dissented. I was personally called a terrorist lover by former military colleagues when I expressed my concern about the vengeful attitudes of some who were invoking scriptural references to the wrath of God as justification for military action. This silence and fear bled also into the halls of our federal legislative branch. Senator Robert Byrd gave a telling speech in the Senate in early 2003 when he said:

> *To contemplate war is to think about the most horrible of human experiences. On this February day, as this nation stands at the brink of battle, every American on some level must be contemplating the horrors of war. Yet, this chamber is, for the most part, silent— ominously, dreadfully silent. There is no debate, no discussion, no attempt to lay out for the nation the pros and cons of this particular war. There is nothing.*

> *We stand passively mute in the United States Senate, paralyzed by our own uncertainty, seemingly stunned by the sheer turmoil of events. Only on the editorial pages of our newspapers is there much substantive discussion*

> *of the prudence or imprudence of engaging in this*
> *particular war. And this is no small conflagration we*
> *contemplate. This is no simple attempt to defang a*
> *villain. No. This coming battle, if it materializes,*
> *represents a turning point in U.S. foreign policy and*
> *possibly a turning point in the recent history of the*
> *world. (Byrd February 12, 2003)*

In September 2001, I had just begun my ministerial internship on the campus of the University of Illinois. I had a discussion on Sunday morning, September 9, with several students who said they didn't have a defining moment in their generation. Forty-eight hours later that moment would come. The history of the world changed course the day a small group of terrorists hijacked four airplanes and crashed them into the financial, military, and (we presume they also intended) the political centers of the American empire.

The term empire is often used pejoratively, but I am using it empirically and dispassionately. The reality is that the United States is a modern world empire. We emerged from the twentieth century and the modern era, after just a few hundred years of worldwide scientific, industrial, military, economic, religious, and socio-cultural revolution, as the globe's dominant force. The United States of America has the power to shape the course of world events. The attacks of September 11, 2001 were simply a catalyst that would set an exercise of that power in motion.

Empires such as ours always have been and likely always will be the object of retaliation by those who feel displaced. Indeed, this nation was founded on revolution against oppression. Five years ago, we were tested and we responded. That response, however, was the predicted, expected, and desired response from the terrorists' perspective. It was reactive, vengeful, retributive, destabilizing, and so far ineffective in both Afghanistan and Iraq. If the United States is to take on the role of world power and empire, then we must be responsible and accountable for our own actions. In time of peace and in the face of inevitable hostility, those nations with the most power need to be proactive, compassionate, restorative, and need to exercise the most restraint. The defining moment of a new generation was nothing more than what psychologists call an activating event. The response to that event and the consequences it holds are what will actually change the world for better or worse. So far, the response has changed the world for the worse and made it a more dangerous place. We have seen an erosion of our own civil rights, the exercise of preemptive war without cause, an increase in international terrorism, an increase in political divisiveness at home, an imbalance of power in our own government, and unprecedented national debt.

Despite the many justifications that have been given for the war in Iraq, which time does not allow me to address sufficiently this morning, I believe the primary purpose was to test the U.S. doctrine and security strategy of preemptive conflict. If you haven't read the 2002 and 2006 National Security Strategies, I suggest you do so. There is much in them that is sound, well thought out, and which, if followed, will lead to a more peaceful world. However, in an era of globalization, one nation's interests cannot be considered independently from others. Our method has become the madness, and is inherently flawed. The current National Security Strategy begins by saying:

> *It is the policy of the United States to seek and support democratic movements and institutions in every nation and culture, with the ultimate goal of ending tyranny in our world. In the world today, the fundamental character of regimes matters as much as the distribution of power among them. The goal of our statecraft is to help create a world of democratic, well-governed states that can meet the needs of their citizens and conduct themselves responsibly in the international system. This is the best way to provide enduring security for the American people. (p. I)*

So, we have declared that democracy is the best form of governance for every society because it promotes freedom. We have established a goal to create a completely democratic world based on this obvious truth. Let's for a minute test this declaration by substituting the word communism for democracy. Those who promoted communism believed that sharing the means of production was the greatest path to ultimate freedom. What if we substituted the words Christianity or Islam? Many Christians and Muslims believe that their religion is the greatest or the only path to salvation. Democracy, done well, does promote human freedom, but what our government has told the rest of the world is that this path is the only path, and that we are determined to impose it upon the rest of the world.

From the perspective of those who oppose the empire of the United States, this is simply fuel for the fire—a fundamentalist and tyrannical declaration for world domination. What's more, is how the passage closes—with a further declaration that democracy is the path by which people around the world should conduct themselves responsibly. King George of England also thought he was telling the people of the newly formed American colonies how to behave responsibly.

Finally, that first paragraph of the National Security Strategy seals the deal against the United States with this non-sequitur: "This is the best way to provide enduring security for the American people." Even if we have convinced others that democracy is the way for them, we are telling them that we don't really care about them or a truly democratic world. Rather, we are just trying to make things safe for ourselves. This is the arrogance that Martin Luther King, Jr. addressed when he said Americans felt they had everything to teach the world and nothing to learn from it (King).

Later, the National Security Strategy recognizes that freedom must be chosen by the people who are oppressed, but continues to speak of only one political continuum from tyranny to democracy. These are not the only two choices for human governance; and even democracy exists in many forms with varying degrees of freedom. Our world-dominating form of capitalist democracy doesn't necessarily appeal to some.

As if this wasn't enough, our National Security Strategy clearly delineates that we reserve the right to use preemptive force to create this free and democratic world. It states:

> The greater the threat, the greater is the risk of inaction—and the more compelling the case for taking anticipatory action to defend ourselves, even if uncertainty remains as to the time and place of the enemy's attack.
>
> To forestall or prevent such hostile acts by our adversaries, the United States will, if necessary, act preemptively in exercising our inherent right of self-defense. The United States will not resort to force in all cases to preempt emerging threats. Our preference is that nonmilitary actions succeed. And no country should ever use preemption as a pretext for aggression. (National Security Strategy 2006, 18)

And yet, preemption as a pretext for aggression is exactly what we have done. In essence, we have told the world that we will attack when we see fit, because we can. This is why we attacked Iraq—because we could. We can't topple the dangerous regimes in North Korea and Iran with military force, even though at times our government's aggressive rhetoric has implied that we could and might. But we could topple Saddam Hussein with military force, and so we did. Why should we expect any less violence or preemption from the rest of the world against us?

The previous National Security Strategy of the United States, published in 2002, began with this statement: "The great struggles of the twentieth century between liberty and totalitarianism ended with a decisive victory for the forces of freedom—and a single sustainable model for national success: freedom, democracy, and free enterprise." (National Security Strategy 2002, Preface) Again, this is a declared single path that we expect every nation in the world to follow. I believe that these "great struggles" between liberty and totalitarianism are at the root of the problem we experience today in defining patriotism, in supporting or opposing war, and in declaring war on terrorism. Americans have substituted the war in Iraq, a preemptive show of force, for their frustration about the attacks of September 11, 2001, and the difficulty of going after an intangible enemy. We wanted the easy certainty of defeating a Mussolini, a Hitler, or the Soviet Communists. But the world isn't that simple.

Throughout the twentieth century, we fought wars of good and evil. We sparred democracy against communism. Dualisms are easy to grasp, easy to convey to the masses, and easy to fight about. Unfortunately, the real world rarely exists as a dualism. Since the end of the Cold War, the world has had a more difficult time grappling with the realities of regional conflicts and wars without physical and national boundaries. Then the events of September 11, 2001 occurred. This enemy was no longer tangible. It was a coalition of anti-Americanism that exists around the globe, and was run by men from several nations who take refuge in several nations. The U.S. government went to Afghanistan to topple a harboring government and to search for a needle in a haystack. Just as a decade of counterterrorism work during the 1990s was unable to bring Osama Bin Laden to justice, so has an overwhelming armed force been unable to defeat this enemy. And so, the U.S. government accused Saddam Hussein of various crimes and United Nations violations and made the case for the war in Iraq. Another nation toppled in the name of democracy. Tragically, neither nation is being rebuilt to the standards that will allow democracy to flourish. If we are to salvage anything from these tragedies, we must rebuild Iraq and Afghanistan as we rebuilt Germany and Japan after World War II. I fear we won't, and that the conditions of these societies will make it difficult for us to do so.

In the meantime, we suffer the erosion of freedom and liberty at home, and we remain silent. In October 2001, Judge Andrew Napolitano, formerly of the New Jersey Supreme Court said:

In a democracy, personal liberties are rarely diminished overnight. Rather, they are lost gradually, by the acts of well-meaning people, with good intentions, amid public approval. But the subtle loss of freedom is never recognized until the crisis is over and we look back in horror. And then it is too late. (Napolitano 184)

Why have we as a nation been so silent and complicit as our government proceeds to world domination? When will it be too late? Our ancestors and predecessors faced this issue when North America was colonized over two-hundred years ago. Well-meaning people escaped oppression and eventually oppressed the indigenous peoples of the Americas in their quest for freedom. Well-meaning people, the founders of this nation included, built a free society based on a declaration and constitution that today remain a model of liberty and justice for the entire world. But they did so with the slave labor of African immigrants and their descendants. We faced the issue of freedom when the slaves were emancipated during a devastating civil war. We faced the issue of freedom when those of European descent moved west and committed one of the greatest genocides of human history, ending barely a hundred years ago. We faced the issue of freedom during World War II when the government incarcerated Japanese Americans. We faced the issue of freedom during McCarthyism and well-meaning attempts to defend the west against Communism. After 100 years of inaction between 1865 and 1964, when the Civil Rights Act was finally passed, we faced issues of freedom again in providing legal rights and protection for non-whites.

When we celebrate our freedom, we must also recognize the abuses against that freedom even when—especially when—those abuses come from within. We must recognize the extreme abuses and costs by which our freedom was attained to ensure that they do not happen again. How will we put into place the cultural revolution that will both reduce the incentive for terrorism and violence, and resolve the problems that are endemic to a society built upon and surviving on violence and oppression as the means to world domination?

As a first practical step, beyond reframing our strategy of world domination through democracy, and eliminating our doctrine of pre-emptive conflict, I believe we must undertake the elimination of all nuclear weaponry. I hope our descendants several generations from now will look upon nuclear weapons and other weapons of mass destruction as a dangerous past chapter in the history of humankind. If post-modern philosophy comes to any conclusion about human behavior, I hope it will be that humans learn there are some things of which we are capable, but in which we simply ought not to engage because the risks are too great. Nuclear, chemical, and biological weapons are such things. Although the threat of mutually assured destruction between the United States and the USSR kept the two from violent conflict on the world stage, the risks and other costs made it too dangerous a game to play. It will take at least many decades, if not centuries, to agree to find and destroy all such weapons, to ban the production of future weapons, and to create and implement even better compliance and verification regimes. But I don't believe we have a choice. Ironically and tragically, I fear we won't actually come to the decision to disarm ourselves as such until after nuclear weapons have been used against us, or used again by us against others.

Another change here at home will be to overcome the cultures of apathy and privilege that pervade our citizenry in their attitudes toward the government. This nation is a democracy in name only. Until seventy, eighty or even ninety percent of the people see fit to vote, we will never have a government of the people, by the people, or for the people. Regardless of who gets elected to any position in this country, they are seldom put into office by more than twenty-five percent of their constituency—usually much less. Getting elected to public office then becomes a game of competing for likely voters and, in some cases, keeping that pool of voters low. This results in increased apathy on the part of the electorate. How will we get the masses interested in the democratic process? I think we need to look beyond the context of voting.

People aren't apathetic about voting. They are apathetic and even cynical about their vote actually making a difference. Americans are cynical because they don't feel a sense of ownership in the process of government. We are focused on enjoying the privileges of this great society, rather making it truly great by working for the plight of the underprivileged at home and abroad. We are cynical not because the problem can't be solved, but because we like being cynical. It's easier than the hard work and sacrifice involved in achieving true democracy and equality at home. Again, we should heed Frederick Douglass's words in thinking about the tyranny of our own government, for this is the context in which he spoke them. "Power concedes nothing without a demand" (Douglass, 579)

John F. Kennedy, Jr. also had such a vision over forty years ago when he created the Peace Corps, and when he said, "Ask not what your country can do for you, but ask what you can do for your country." (President Kennedy's Inaugural Address, 1961) These words are not empty, idealistic pie in the sky. This is true patriotism. Patriotism is not dictated and legislated through fear, but offered as an opportunity to change the world around you.

Next, we must heed the lessons learned from the Vietnam War, the Korean War, and World War II, sparing no expense in ensuring that our returning soldiers, sailors, airmen, and marines, and their families have every necessary tool at their disposal to continue their lives beyond Iraq. I believe the best moral stance we can take concerning war is to oppose its conduct, but to offer every measure of support to those who must fight when necessary. Thousands of families have lost loved ones in this war. Tens of thousands more are watching their loved ones return home with post-traumatic stress disorder at least, and more often with severe physical and mental disabilities. This war has already perpetuated the systems of injustice at home that will further stress our health care and criminal justice systems. We should demand that our government guarantee educational, employment, and housing opportunities to our veterans and their families—the best education, and the best mental and physical health care that the world has to offer. I find it no coincidence that our current health care crisis and the ten-fold increase in incarceration in this country coincided with the conduct and the aftermath of the Vietnam War. We have a tragic tendency in the United States to put people into the worst of circumstances and then to condemn them when they fail. Let us not make this mistake again. Let us use this tragedy as an opportunity to do the right thing, not only for our veterans, but for all people.

Of course, we must demand an end to the occupation in Iraq. Because of the repeated failures to date to adequately train the Iraqi military and police forces, and because there is no incentive for Iraqis not to engage in civil war, this will be a particularly difficult and slow task.

What will the world look like beyond Iraq? If we, as people of conscience concerned not only with our own security, but that of the entire world, demand a change of course, then democracy and freedom will have a chance to prevail. If we allow our government to continue its path of imposing democracy with military force as it sees fit, then I fear we cannot even imagine the repercussions.

In the prophetic words of Maya Angelou,

> *History, despite its wrenching pain,*
> *Cannot be unlived, but if faced*
> *With courage, need not be lived again. ...*
> *Women, children, men,*
> *Take it into the palms of your hands,*
> *Mold it into the shape of your most*
> *Private need. Sculpt it into*
> *The image of your most public self.*
> *Lift up your hearts*
> *Each new hour holds new chances*
> *For a new beginning.*
> *Do not be wedded forever*
> *To fear, yoked eternally*
> *To brutishness ...*

Here on the pulse of this new day
You may have the grace to look up and out
And into your sister's eyes,
And into your brother's face,
Your country,
And say simply
Very simply
With hope—
Good morning.

BIBLIOGRAPHY

Americans with Disabilities Act, 101st Cong. (1990), 2nd sess., 3. US Statutes at Large, vol. 104, p. 329

Angelou, Maya. On the Pulse of Morning (New York: Random House, 1993). [Inaugural Poem read by the poet at the Presidential Inauguration of William Jefferson Clinton on January 20, 1993]

Berry, Wendell. "The Peace of Wild Things." The Selected Poems of Wendell Berry. Washington D.C. : Counterpoint, 1998. p. 30.

Bittner, Mark. The Wild Parrots of Telegraph Hill. New York: Harmony Books, 2004.

Byrd, Senator Robert of West Virginia speaking to an Executive Session of the U.S. Senate on February 12, 2003. Congressional Record - Senate. 108th Cong., p. S2268. [Searchable online at http:// thomas.loc.gov/home/ r108query.html]

CNN, http://www.cnn.com/interactive/us/0503/gallery.schiavo.reax/ content .1.html

Douglass, Frederick [1857] (1985). "The Significance of Emancipation in the West Indies." Speech, Canandaigua, New York, August 3, 1857; collected in pamphlet by author. In The Frederick Douglass Papers. Series One: Speeches, Debates, and Interviews. Volume 3: 1855-63. Edited by John W. Blassingame. New Haven: Yale University Press, p. 204. [This quote exists in various versions. The version used here is from the Unitarian Universalist Association, Singing the Living Tradition (Boston: Author, 1993), 579.]

Eisland, Nancy. The Disabled God: Toward a Liberatory Theology of Disability (Nashville: Abingdon Press, 1994) p. 67

Holmes, Stephen. New York Times, September 30, 1991, A8

Kennedy, Jr., John F. Inaugural Address, Washington, DC, January 20, 1961.

King, Jr., Martin Luther. "Beyond Vietnam" in Clayborne Carson and Kris Shepard, eds. A Call to Conscience: The Landmark Speeches of Dr. Martin Luther King, Jr. (New York: IPM/Warner Books, 2001). [Dr. King delivered this speech on April 4, 1967 at Riverside Church in New York City. It is available online at: http://www.stanford.edu/group/ King/mlkpapers/]

Lach, William, Ed. A Green Sound. Boston: Skinner House Books, 1992. p. 37.

Manker-Seale, Rev. Susan. The Moral Arc of the Universe: Bending Toward Justice. Sermon, January 15, 2006. Online at http://www.uucnwt.org/sermons/TheMoralArcOfTheUniverse%201-15-06.html.

McNatt, Rosemary Bray. Paraphrase of Coretta Scott King, "To Pray Without Apology: Why Martin Luther King Jr.   Wasn't a Unitarian Universalist." UU World. November/December 2002.

Napolitano, Andrew. "Don't Tread on Freedom," New Jersey Law Journal 166 (October 15, 2001): 184.

National Security Strategy of the United States of America. The White

House, Washington, DC (March 2006), p.I. [Available online at: http://www.whitehouse.gov/nsc/nss/2006/]

National Security Strategy of the United States of America. The White House, Washington, DC (September 2002), Preface. [Available online at: http://www.whitehouse.gov/nsc/nss/2002/]

Salbi, Zainab. The Other Side of War: Women's Stories of Survival and Hope. National Geographic Press. 2006.

Southworth, Bruce. At Home in Creativity. Boston, MA: Skinner House Books, 1995.

Wieman, Henry Nelson. The Source of Human Good. Chicago, IL: The University of Chicago Press, 1946.

About The Authors

Stephen Atkinson, MDiv '07, is the newly-called minister of North Shore Unitarian Church in West Vancouver, British Columbia, Canada.

As a "thirty-something," **Alice Blair Wesley** was an independent (non-credit) student at Meadville Lombard from 1973-77 while she also did graduate work at Lamar University in Beaumont, Texas, in preparation for ministry. For 20 years she served UU congregations in Texas, Maryland and New Jersey. She retired from the parish in 1996 and now lives alternately in Allentown, Pennsylvania and Bellevue, Washington. Alice has written theological papers for delivery at many summer institutes, at ministers' study groups, retreats, convocations and chapter meetings, and at District Annual Meetings and General Assemblies. Her books, Myths of Time and History and Our Covenant, have been widely used as a text in church study groups, and the latter in seminary courses on UU history and polity. Both are published lecture series, the first given during a week at Ferry Beach in 1985 and the other as the Minns Lectures of 2000-01.

Anne Barker is a Canadian candidate for Unitarian Universalist Ministry, mother of two teenage sons, and passionate appreciator of the diversity of human experience.

David E. Bumbaugh, BD '64, Minister Emeritus of the Unitarian Church in Summit, New Jersey, is Professor of Ministry at Meadville Lombard Theological School. He is the author of The Education of

God and Unitarian Universalism: A Narrative History, and chapters in A Language of Reverence, Narnia Revisited, A Bold Experiment, and Experiencing Poverty.

Eliza Galaher, MDiv ' 07, is a newly-settled minister at Wildflower Church in Austin, Texas.

India McCanse is in her third year of studies at Meadville Lombard. She holds Bachelor's and Master's degrees in counseling psychology. McCanse spent 22 years in nonprofit leadership serving Planned Parenthood, Big Brothers Big Sisters and other organizations. McCanse has received numerous honors and awards including a scholarship to a summer program at the Harvard Business School. A third generation Unitarian Universalist, McCanse has left her human service career to pursue ministry full time. She lives with her two beloved canines in Milwaukee, Wisconsin.

Aaron McEmrys, MDiv '07, is the Interim Assistant Minister, Director of Social Justice and of Youth and Young Adult Ministries, First Universalist Church of Denver.

Justin Osterman, DMin '99, is minister of the Central Unitarian Church in Paramus, New Jersey. He is a lifelong Unitarian Universalist, a former US Army paratrooper, and President of Meadville Lombard Theological School's Alumni/ae Association.

David Pyle is a third year MDiv student, and currently the Ministerial Intern at the Unitarian Church of Evanston, IL. He is also a student of Ven. Robert Joshin Althouse in the White Plum line of Zen, and a member of the Empty Sound Zen Temple in Oak Park, Illinois. A 2nd Lieutenant in the United States Army, David is serving as an Army Chaplain Candidate. This essay was written as a part of a class taught by Rev. James Ishmael Ford Roshi.

Jessica Purple Rodela is a fourth-year MDiv student. Before entering seminary, she worked as an English teacher, actress, logistics analyst, and freelance writer. In 2007, she won the St. Lawrence Foundation Essay Award and second prize in the Richard Borden and Paul Holton Awards for Sermonic Excellence. She is the featured writer for *Equal Measure: Portraits of Love*, a photography exhibit on marriage equality in Buffalo, New York.

Tracy Springberry lives in Spokane, Washington with her partner and three sons. She has an MA in creative non-fiction, has published essays in *The Sun*, *The Christian Science Monitor* and other publications and is the co-editor of *At Work in Life's Garden: Writers on the Spiritual Adventure of Parenting*. She is a student in the Modified Residency Program at Meadville Lombard Theological School.

Matt Tittle, MDiv '04, is Minister of the Bay Area Unitarian Universalist Church in Houston, Texas. He is a retired naval officer, former university professor, and author of *Taking Back Faith: Heretical Thoughts for a New Century.*

www.ingramcontent.com/pod-product-compliance
Lightning Source LLC
Chambersburg PA
CBHW060941050726
47592CB00003B/1046